M000202751

HEART ATTACHMENTS

*How what you love shapes your thinking,
behaviors and destiny*

BRUCE J. HAMMOND

Heart Attachments
Copyright © 2020 Bruce Hammond
All rights reserved.
ISBN 13:978-1-7346245-1-9 (paperback)
ISBN 13: 978-1-7346245-0-2(ebook)

Unless otherwise identified, Scripture quotations are taken from the New American Standard Bible®, Copyright ©1960,1962,1963,1968,1971,1972,1973,1975,1977,1995by The Lockman Foundation. Used by permission. www.Lockman.org. Scriptures marked *NIV* are taken from Holy Bible, New International Version®, NIV® Copyright © 1973, 1978, 1984, 2011 by Biblica, Inc.® Used by permission. All rights reserved worldwide.Scriptures marked *KJV* are taken from The King James Version of the Holy Bible. Public Domain. Scriptures marked *AMP* are taken from the Amplified® Bible, Copyright © 2015 by The Lockman Foundation. Used by permission. www.Lockman.org. Scriptures marked *HCSB* are taken from Holman Christian Standard Bible®, Copyright © 1999, 2000, 2002, 2003, 2009 by Holman Bible Publishers. Used by permission. Scriptures marked *NLT* are taken from the Holy Bible, New Living Translation, copyright © 1996, 2004, 2015 by Tyndale House Foundation. Used by permission of Tyndale House Publishers, Inc., Carol Stream, Illinois 60188. All rights reserved.Scriptures marked *ISV* are taken from International Standard Version, copyright© 1996-2008 by the ISV Foundation. All rights reserved internationally. Scriptures marked *NKJV* are taken from the New King James Version®. Copyright© 1982 by Thomas Nelson, Inc. Used by permission. All rights reserved. Scriptures marked *ESV* are taken from the The Holy Bible, English Standard Version ® Copyright© 2001 by Crossway, a publishing ministry of Good News Publishers. Used by permission. Scriptures marked *Phillips* are taken from The New Testament in Modern English by J.B Phillips copyright © 1960, 1972 J. B. Phillips. Administered by The Archbishops' Council of the Church of England. Used by Permission.

Library of Congress Control Number: 2018675309
Photo by Constant Loubier on Unsplash
Published by Bruce Hammond. Nashville, Tn
.www.heartattachment.com

Table of Contents

ACKNOWLEDGEMENTS

I'd like to thank my wife, Jean. She not only helped with writing and artistic design, but her life was an inspiration for many of the elements of this book.

I want to thank Hannah Anderson Krog for her skillful editing of this book. She was both patient and precise in revising the text and offering suggestions. I'm grateful for her kindness and willingness to give so much time to this work.

Thanks to Sue Gibson for proofreading and for her wonderful words of encouragement during the editing process.

I am indebted to my mother, Elsa Hammond. She was an invaluable resource on the artistic aspects of the book.

Finally, my appreciation goes out to those people who allowed me to share their "case studies." I think their stories will bring clarity to the themes of this book. Their names have been changed, and I've made some alterations to their accounts to protect their identities.

INTRODUCTION

Some years ago, God began doing a transformative work in the lives of my wife Jean and I. He started uncovering damaged emotions, wrong thinking, and false beliefs we held.

We had all kinds of misconceptions about ourselves and God. For instance, we didn't feel valuable unless we were fulfilling specific standards. This was not a conscious belief system. In fact, our Christian theology told us we were made in God's image, Jesus had paid for our sins and loved us unconditionally, and we had intrinsic value. Nevertheless, there was an unsettled feeling that we were not accepted by God or people unless we lived up to certain criteria.

Both of us had deeply ingrained thought patterns. Our thoughts seemed to track a particular direction, and no matter what we did, these thoughts persisted. It was like having a computer program in our minds telling us what our lives needed to look like to be significant, what our spouse was required to do for us to feel safe, and what would give us true satisfaction.

Simply identifying our wrong thinking didn't seem to be the answer. We realized something deeper was required; our inner life needed renovation.

We had so many questions for God: How would we positively change our thinking, heal our emotions, rightly align our beliefs, and change our behaviors? It came as a bit of a surprise to find out that God's answer wasn't some system or a 5-step program.

Through the pages of this book, we will share the answer that God gave us. Jean and I started a ministry to help people, using the insights and tools God provided for us on our journey. We've seen countless people set free, delivered, and restored. This book will discuss what we learned, how Jesus Christ transformed us, and how we've seen Him change the lives of others.

CHAPTER ONE

THE THREE FACULTIES

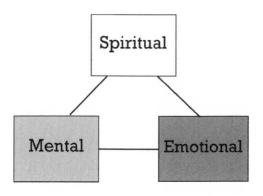

Let's begin by looking at what I call "the three faculties": mental, spiritual, and emotional. Understanding these faculties is key to walking a balanced life and, more importantly, in relating to God and people. The three faculties come to knowledge differently, function uniquely, and have varying strengths and weaknesses. They operate individually but also are meant to work together in balance and unity. When the faculties are fully functioning in their proper boundaries, there is a beautiful clarity, flow, and balance within us.

Dysfunction exists when a faculty is overused or underused. For instance, if we only use our mental faculty, we may know about God but not know Him in a living and personal way. We must also engage the spiritual and emotional faculties to have an intimate, transforming relationship with God.

One of the faculties may know something to be true, while another does not. We may know something in our mind and spirit but not in our emotions.

For example, take the Biblical concept of "sonship." The Bible says that when we receive and trust in Jesus, we become a son or daughter of God.

> **John 1:12**: *But as many as received Him, to them He gave the right to become children of God.*

Receiving and believing in Jesus involves all three faculties; it is a mental, spiritual, and emotional process. When we trust in Jesus, we are "born again" and take on a new nature; it's a life-altering experience.

> **1 Peter 1:23**: *For you have been born again not of seed which is perishable but imperishable, that is, through the living and enduring word of God.*

But at some point, believers may question whether they are indeed a child of God. Often this is due to a lack of *emotional* knowledge of this truth.

How does this play out? Let's say a believer reads the following verse:

Galatians 3:26: *For you are all sons of God through faith in Christ Jesus.*

As they think about the meaning of this verse, they mentally understand the truth that they are a child of God. They think, "I have trusted in Jesus for my salvation and have received Him; therefore, I am God's son." This knowledge is acquired by reason.

As they are reading about and pondering sonship, the Spirit of God "testifies" in their spiritual faculty that they are a child of God.

Romans 8:16: *The Spirit Himself testifies with our spirit that we are children of God.*

This spiritual knowledge is perceived through their spiritual faculty; it is understood intuitively by the Holy Spirit's revelation to their spirit.

But there may be a nagging feeling, an emotional doubt whether they really are a son.

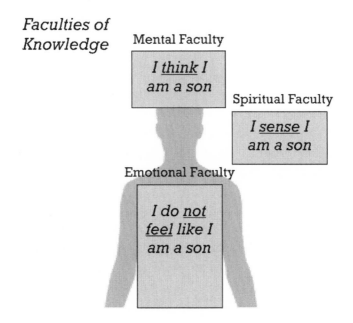

Someone may have accurate theology and mental knowledge about their sonship but still not *feel* like a son. They haven't experienced their sonship, so they don't know it emotionally.

People often have persistent doubts about God's character and find it difficult to trust Him because they haven't come to know Him emotionally. These doubts are not due to a lack of intellectual or spiritual knowledge but a lack of emotional knowledge.

Some might say it doesn't really matter what we feel. But it does! In fact, unresolved issues of the heart often end up dominating our lives. Unconsciously, we will look for ways to fill emotional deficits.

This brings us to an important question: How does a faculty come to know things?

There is actually a branch of philosophy that studies the nature and origin of knowledge, which is called "epistemology." Epistemology asks the question, "How do we know what we know?"[1] Epistemology comes into play with the three faculties, because each has a unique way it comes to knowledge. The mind knows through reason, the spirit through revelation, and the emotions through relationship.

At one time, I thought there were two kinds of knowledge: mental and spiritual. But then I found another type of knowledge on my journey: emotional knowledge. This is knowledge flowing from a relationship, rather than a mental process or spiritual perception.

When I was first confronted with the concept of emotional knowledge, I was puzzled, to say the least. I found myself unable to function in this new-found territory. It was as if someone had given me a new car, but I couldn't get inside to give it a test run. My emotional intelligence was about as low as it could get. But as I learned to operate more "from the heart," I found my relationships with God and people deepened.

It is important to mentally and spiritually comprehend what Scripture says, but we also need to experientially know Jesus, who is the living, breathing Word of God.

John 1:14: *And the Word became flesh, and dwelt among us, and we saw His glory, glory as of the only begotten from the Father, full of grace and truth.*

As we relate to God and *experience* Him, we will acquire emotional knowledge, and this brings balance and health to our souls.

Although each faculty has distinct and individual operations, they also influence one another. There is a powerful principle at work within the human soul, what I call *the heart leading the head*. Generally speaking, things start in the emotions and then move into our thinking.

This means *negative* things like bad character (Matt.15:19), idolatry, wounding, and deficits, originate in the heart and then affect the mind. Also, *positive* things like good character, love for God, transformation (2 Cor. 3:18), and renewal (Rom. 12:2), begin in the emotional faculty and then work their way into the mental faculty. Renewal of the mind *follows* the transformation of the emotions (Eph. 4:23).

Now let's look at how these faculties work, their strengths and weakness, how they interrelate, and how they arrive at knowledge.

Mental Faculty "I think"

God is rational and has made us in His image, with the ability to reason.

> ***Isaiah 1:18:*** *"Come now, and let us **reason** together," says the LORD. "Though your sins are as scarlet, they will be as white as snow; Though they are red like crimson, they will be like wool." (emphasis added)*

The mental faculty assesses, compares, and contrasts data and stores information. It is particularly good at logic. For instance, if all dogs are mammals, and I have a dog named Rover, I can make a reasonable deduction that Rover is a mammal. The other faculties may come to know similar things, but not by logical reasoning.

Another function of the mind is that of a gatekeeper for the other faculties. In this role, the mind filters out the bad and opens the door to the good. What our minds meditate on influences our emotions and spirit. This is why Scripture tells us to "think on" certain things:

Philippians 4:8: *Finally, brethren, whatsoever things are true, whatsoever things are honest, whatsoever things are just, whatsoever things are pure, whatsoever things are lovely, whatsoever things are of good report; if there be any virtue, and if there be any praise,* **think on** *these things. (KJV -emphasis added)*

The mind is also a stabilizer. If our spiritual perceptions become unclear (1 Cor. 13:12), we can find truth by focusing on the written Word of God. This gives us context and boundaries to what we perceive in our spiritual faculty.

Our mental faculty also helps our emotional faculty. Thinking about things that are good and "lovely" will have a positive effect on our emotions. Or focusing our minds on an attribute of God, like His *faithfulness,* can comfort and strengthen us emotionally.

Contrary to Eastern religions, where the goal is to empty the mind, in Christianity, the mind plays a vital role in collaboration with the other faculties. Christianity has an excellent quality in that it is grounded in historical, objective facts.So, our faith in Jesus includes mental knowledge.

Rather than diminishing the role of the mental faculty, the Apostle Paul admonishes us to allow God to "renew" our minds.

Romans 12:2: *And do not be conformed to this world, but be transformed by the* **renewing of your mind,** *so* *that you may prove what the will of God is, that which is good and acceptable and perfect. (emphasis added)*

Throughout the Scriptures, we are advised to use our mental faculty. We are told to: "remember" (Deut. 24:18), "consider" (1 Sam. 12:24), "think on" (Phil. 4:8), "reason" (Isa. 1:18), and "study" (2 Tim. 2:15). All of these are mental functions.

We are even admonished to "love God with our minds" (Mark 12:30) and to "set" our minds toward heaven (Col. 3:2).

The mind has a malleable quality whereby it can be *strengthened*. This is not just an ability to comprehend or store information but a capacity to be built up like a muscle that is strengthened through exercise.

For instance, remaining focused during pressure-filled situations or being mentally determined to make it through difficulties develops mental strength.

God told the prophet Ezekiel that He would make his "forehead like a stone." Ezekiel's firmness of mind was necessary because of the resistance he would face.

Ezekiel 3:8-9: *Behold, I have made your face as hard as their faces and your forehead as hard as their foreheads. I will make your forehead like the hardest stone, harder than flint. Do not be afraid of them or terrified by them, though they are a rebellious people. (NIV)*

My background is in aviation. A strong mind is an essential quality for a professional pilot because the job demands mental focus amid stressful situations.

I remember cruising along in a Learjet at 39,000 feet when suddenly both generators failed. At this moment, I realized there were only 30 minutes of electricity left, and then I would not be able to navigate the aircraft. My co-pilot and I frantically ran through a complicated checklist, descended rapidly, worked the radios, and looked for a suitable airport. It seemed like my emotions were going to overtake me like a giant wave. To make matters worse, it was a rainy day with low visibility. But I had to stay calm and mentally strong, traits developed through training and experience. Fortunately, we landed the aircraft just in time.

To prepare for these kinds of situations, pilots endure training in simulators, which is a kind of mental weightlifting to strengthen the muscles of their minds. They practice remaining focused, clear-headed, and decisive when confronted with an array of emergencies and system failures. These stressful simulations help pilots develop a mental fortitude that gets them through crises in the real world and prevents them from "fainting in the day of adversity" (Prov. 24:10).

The Apostle Paul had mental focus as he set out to "lay hold" of Christ Jesus. He strove to "forget" what was behind and "press on" toward the goal of meeting and becoming like the Lord Jesus.

Philippians 3:13-14: Brethren, I do not regard myself as having laid hold of it yet; but one thing I do: forgetting what lies behind and reaching forward to what lies ahead, I press on toward the goal for the prize of the upward call of God in Christ Jesus.

Because the mind is such a powerful tool, it is understandable that many rely on it too much. But it has limits and needs to be used in concert with the other faculties. Balanced use of the three facilities will keep us anchored in rational truth while experiencing a life-flow that comes from the spiritual and emotional faculties.

Spiritual Faculty – "I sense"

With the spiritual faculty, we perceive the spirit realm and communicate with God. This perception is not so much a feeling as it is a sense.

In addition to giving us perception into the spiritual world, our spiritual faculty is the point of contact with the Holy Spirit. God's Spirit "testifies" to certain truths with the spirit of man.

> **Romans 8:16:** *The Spirit Himself testifies with our spirit that we are children of God.*

> **Galatians 4:6:** *Because you are sons, God has sent forth the Spirit of His Son into our hearts, crying, "Abba! Father!"*

> **1 John 2:20**: *But you have an anointing from the Holy One, and all of you know the truth. (NIV)*

Knowledge comes to the spiritual faculty as the Holy Spirit testifies to fundamental truths about sonship and salvation. But the Holy Spirit does more than verify these facts. He brings comfort (John 15:26), direction (Acts 8:29), insight (John 16:13), wisdom (1 Cor.12:8), and illumination to our reading of Scripture (John 14:26, Ps.119:18), and he helps us discern spiritual realities (1 Cor. 2:13).

The Bible gives us wisdom and principles, but the Holy Spirit, communicating with our spiritual faculty, applies God's wisdom and knowledge to the daily details of our lives.

This communication or spiritual perception might be completely unrelated to anything the mind observes. Sometimes before a rational deduction is made, we can have a "gut-feeling" or intuition about a particular fact.

And at times, this spiritual sense will be contrary to what we feel. The spiritual and emotional faculties have distinct operations and know things differently. They are not always in agreement.

Our spiritual sense can lead us directly to the truth, sometimes without any verification from the other faculties. Often I've sensed something to be accurate without knowing where the information came from; the knowledge seemed to have dropped in from nowhere. It was strictly a spiritual impression from the Holy Spirit.

Learning to hear the voice of God and developing spiritual perception is fine-tuned with use. Training our spiritual senses does not happen overnight; just like any process of maturation, it can take some time and practice.

*Hebrews 5:14: But solid food is for **the mature**, who because of **practice** have their **senses trained** to discern good. (emphasis added)*

The spiritual faculty should function side-by-side with the other faculties. Sometimes there are inaccuracies in what we are sensing, and the other faculties can bring balance. For instance, we can mentally find truth by referring to the written Word of God, verifying things with our five senses, or by listening to the counsel of others.

Proverbs 11:14: Where there is no guidance the people fall, but in abundance of counselors there is victory.

The emotional faculty can also help. If we have an emotional understanding of God's nature, we can discern inaccuracies in our spiritual perceptions. Having emotional knowledge of God's excellency of character – His kindness, goodness, holiness, and righteousness – helps us identify and disregard any false spiritual impressions about Him.

Through the spiritual faculty, we can actually experience God. A Greek word that describes this kind of first-hand, experiential knowing is "ginóskó." It is used more than 200 times in the New Testament, highlighting the importance of experiential knowledge.[2]

The spiritual faculty is an important communication link to God. The Holy Spirit gives us "wisdom and revelation" via this faculty so we can have an experiential, intimate knowledge of His person.

Ephesians 1:17: *I keep asking that the God of our Lord Jesus Christ, the glorious Father, may give you the* **Spirit of wisdom and revelation, so that you may** <u>**know**</u> **[epignósis –experiential, participatory knowledge] him better.** *(NIV -emphasis, brackets added)*

Emotional Faculty "I feel"

The emotional faculty is generally the most misunderstood. Christians often teach that emotions should be at the back of the proverbial train, never pulling the train. Emotions are stigmatized frequently as faulty, unreliable, and dangerous. Some people believe that any expression of emotion is ungodly.

All three faculties are important for a healthy life with God and others. However, it is the often-neglected emotional faculty that plays a central role in relationships, soul transformation, emotional health, motivation, behavior, and spiritual maturity.

The emotional faculty is ground zero because Scripture says everything we do flows from our hearts.

Proverbs 4:23: *Above all else, guard your heart, for everything you do flows from it. (NIV)*

We must pay attention to our hearts. There is an intense war being waged between God, who desires to impart His security into this heart soil, and a dark enemy, whose goal is to sow weeds into this ground to torment, enslave, and destroy us (John 10:10, 1 Pet. 5:8).

Much of the misunderstanding about this faculty stems from a narrow view of what "emotions" are. The emotional faculty is more than just feelings. Through this faculty, we also believe, choose, relate, experience, desire, value, love, and have our sense of self.

Over the long haul, the emotional faculty is the primary driver in how we think and behave. Any unfinished business in the emotional realm will spill over into the other faculties and areas of life. In reality, emotions influence our thinking and behavior at an unconscious level more than we realize.

The emotional faculty is also a receptor, taking in experiences and relational impartations. Like a container, it's filled with good and bad relational experiences, or it can be left empty due to a lack of relational experiences. And experiences and impartations stay with us; they don't go away with time. The saying "time heals all wounds" is not true. Emotional wounds remain until healing occurs and there are positive relational impartations.

Emotional Impartations

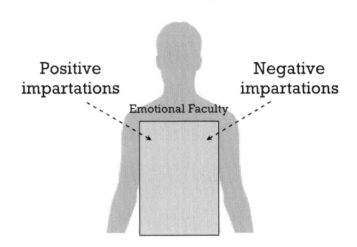

Positive impartations

Negative impartations

Emotional Faculty

Like the mind, the emotional faculty stores knowledge, but it is knowledge of a different sort. It stores experiences, both positive and negative. And more specifically, it stores relational experiences.

The emotions can also mature and are transformed by knowing God. The emotional faculty comes to knowledge through experience and relationship. "Epignósis" (or its verbal form "epiginóskó") is a Greek word the Bible uses for knowledge that is experiential and *participatory*.

Vines Expository Dictionary defines epignósis in this way:

expressing a fuller or a full "knowledge," a greater participation by the "knower" in the object "known," thus more powerfully influencing him.[3]

In epignósis knowledge, the Bride of Christ (the knower) participates in the knowledge of the Bridegroom Jesus (the object).

The Bride participates by loving, worshiping, and relating with her Bridegroom. It is through loving communion and oneness that Christ reveals Himself to us. The emotional faculty acquires knowledge by this kind of person-to-person interaction.

2 Peter: 1:2-3: *...and peace be multiplied to you in the* **knowledge** *[epignósis] of God and of Jesus our Lord; seeing that His divine power has granted to us everything pertaining to life and godliness, through the true* **knowledge** *[epignósis] of Him who called us by His own glory and excellence. (emphasis, brackets added)*

Similar to the mental faculty, the emotional faculty can be strengthened. Emotional muscles develop through resistance, which comes through difficult situations and trials. Inner strength is worked into the emotional faculty through perseverance.

The Christian is never alone when going through various trials and tribulations. The Spirit of God works within, strengthening their emotional faculty, or "inner man."

Ephesians 3:16: *...that He would grant you, according to the riches of His glory, to be* **strengthened** *with power* **through His Spirit in the inner man** *(emphasis added)*

As you can see, there is much more to the emotional faculty than just feeling certain emotions. It's worth understanding how this vast and multi-faceted part of our being operates. Our relationships with God and other people are enriched when we become proficient in using this faculty. God has given us the emotional faculty so we might experience His person, so we can taste that He is good.

Psalm 34:8: *Taste and see that the LORD is good; blessed is the one who takes refuge in him. (NIV)*

Overuse of the Mental Faculty

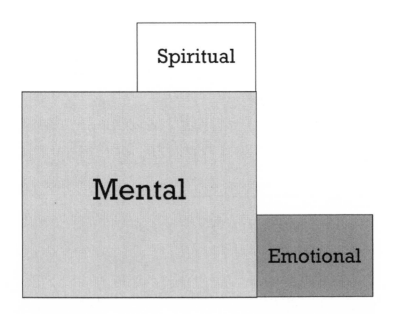

Some people overuse their mental faculty and suppress the emotional or spiritual parts of their being. In my life, this was the case. I believed emotions were unruly and needed to be reined in by cool, objective thinking.

But then I had a life-altering season that turned my view of emotions upside-down. In my late 20s, several friends independently confronted me with a similar statement: "nobody knows you." It felt like an intervention as they came, one-by-one, to set me straight.

Their comments confused me. I was part of a large community, and as far I could tell, many people "knew" me. My friends then persisted with uncomfortable questions about how I felt about specific issues. Inwardly, I thought, "Who cares what I feel? What difference does it make?"

But these folks were light years ahead of me. They understood something I did not: we have to share from our core, from our emotional faculty, to truly be known as a person. I had to open the doors to my heart so people could see the real me. This meant expressing my feelings: what made me glad, sad, and mad, as well as my values, inspirations, and dreams.

Did this take vulnerability? Absolutely! But it was worth the risk because an amazing thing happened when I finally relented and gave my inquiring friends a glimpse of my inner world. For the first time in my life, I genuinely felt known. I was no longer isolated and alone inside myself.

This simple act of opening up and revealing my emotions made me feel like Dorothy in the Wizard of Oz as she stepped from black and white into technicolor. I was in a different land, learning to speak a new language: the language of the emotional faculty.

I'm not alone when it comes to overusing the mental faculty. Western culture is rooted in a Greek worldview, which exalts the intellect and downplays the spiritual and emotional realms.

Does this mean we should abandon our cognitive abilities altogether? No, but there's a tendency in all of us, stemming from the fall of man (Gen. 3:5-6), to trust in our natural reason and five senses beyond their designed capacity.

Mental knowledge can become an idol if we depend on it too much. God may throw us a curveball to dethrone our idolatry of the mind by clouding our path. When the road is obscured and we can't logically determine our next steps, we come back to faith in God and His character. Or the Holy Spirit may communicate something into our spirits, such as a direction or a vision, which might not make sense to our finite minds. Again, this requires trust in God over our intellect.

Obtaining mental knowledge can also be a way of exalting ourselves. The Apostle Paul makes the point that mental knowledge makes one "arrogant," but "love edifies."

> *1 Corinthians 8:1: Now concerning things sacrificed to idols, we know that we all have knowledge. **Knowledge makes arrogant, but love edifies.** (emphasis added)*

Adam and Eve were given full liberty to eat from the "tree of life," which meant they could experience a life-giving relationship with God. But they were not to go after mental knowledge, independent of God, by eating from the "tree of knowledge of good and evil" (Gen. 2:16-17).

The serpent tempted Eve to eat from the forbidden tree, by telling her this knowledge would make her "like God." Instead of eating from the tree of life and getting life from God, she and Adam ate the fruit from the tree of knowledge of good and evil to exalt themselves.

> *Genesis 3:4-5: The serpent said to the woman, "You surely will not die! For God knows that in the day you eat from it your eyes will be opened, and you will be **like God**, knowing good and evil. When the woman saw that*

*the tree was good for food, and that it was a delight to the eyes, and that the tree was desirable to make one **wise**, she took from its fruit and ate; and she gave also to her husband with her, and he ate. (emphasis added)*

But there was no life in this autonomous wisdom. Life is in God; it flows from a heart attachment to Him.

Revelation 22:1-2: *Then he showed me a river of the **water of life**, clear as crystal, **coming from the throne of God and of the Lamb,** in the middle of its street. On either side of the river was **the tree of life,** bearing twelve kinds of fruit, yielding its fruit every month; and the leaves of the tree were for the healing of the nations. (emphasis added)*

We really can't experience God with mental knowledge only. Life comes from the *experiential* knowledge of God's person, which requires the spiritual and emotional faculties.

John 17:3: *This is eternal life, that they may **know** [ginóskó – experiential knowing] You, the only true God, and Jesus Christ whom You have sent. (emphasis, brackets added)*

The mind also has another profound limitation. God has established a principle within us where the heart leads the head. What (or who) we choose to believe, trust, worship, and embrace from the heart will ultimately shape our thinking and, in turn, our behavior.

If we trust in *money*, a thought pattern will develop that says money is the answer to everything. Or if we are attached to *success*, it will consume our thoughts.

25

Of course, there are times when our head leads our heart and we make decisions solely based on logic. But over time, our head will align with the attachments of our heart.

So, this means if we have a heart attachment to God and experience Him, it positively affects our thinking. Being emotionally "rooted and grounded in love" allows for greater mental "comprehension" and clarity of thought.

*Ephesians 3:17-18: ...so that Christ may dwell in your hearts through faith; and that you, being **rooted and grounded in <u>love</u>**, may be able to **<u>comprehend</u>** with all the saints what is the breadth and length and height and depth... (emphasis added)*

Overuse of the Spiritual Faculty

26

To think we can actually communicate with the God of the universe is pretty amazing stuff. And when we realize there's a link to the fascinating and exciting realm of the spirit, overusing the spiritual faculty can be a real temptation. This is especially true for those personality types who are naturally more intuitive and seem to have been born with a sensitive spiritual antenna.

In saying *overuse* of the spiritual faculty, I am not speaking about the activity of the Holy Spirit of God in and through us, which is in *God's* hands (John 3:8). Nor am I focusing on the importance of allowing the Holy Spirit to be the *governor* of our lives. I am concentrating on *our* responsibilities when it comes to using our spiritual faculty and the boundaries that need to be in place to maintain a healthy balance with the other faculties.

The Apostle Paul tells us that when we are sensing the Holy Spirit, we have control of our spiritual faculty and are responsible for its operations; it is "subject" to us.

1 Corinthians 14:32: ...and the spirits of prophets are subject to prophets.

Some limitations go with the spiritual faculty's operations: we only know "in part" (1 Cor. 13:12, KJV), hear a "still small voice" (1 Kings 19:12, KJV), and see things "through a glass darkly" (1 Cor. 13:12, KJV).

So, we need to keep the other faculties in the mix and not trust everything our spiritual perceptions tell us. Paul has us holding what is "good" in our prophetic perceptions, meaning there may be inaccuracies in what we sense.

*1 Thessalonians 5:20-21: ...do not despise prophetic utterances. **But examine everything carefully; hold fast to that which is good.** (emphasis added)*

27

While it is true that God communicates regularly through the spiritual faculty, we become vulnerable to deception if we believe this is the *only* way we hear from Him.

Speaking from experience, at one point, I was so focused on perceiving the Spirit of God, that things got really messy. At the time, using my spiritual perception seemed to be the best way to be safe, secure, and in God's perfect will. But there was an underlying problem. I had a wrong concept of God's nature, a problem rooted in my emotional faculty. Because my father was often harsh with me, I was wounded emotionally. This damage in my soul twisted my understanding of God's character.

I wrongly believed that if I could hear God precisely, and do what He said, He wouldn't treat me harshly. This striving to discern God's directives became a kind of compulsion. I turned spiritual perception into a defense mechanism as I tried to stay in line with God by hearing and following His every instruction. But I was making spiritual discernment my god. Spiritual communication became an idol, as I became overly dependent and overly confident in what it could do for me.

God would later restore my emotions when I became dependent on Him, rather than my ability to discern His voice. In fact, the Holy Spirit did much emotional healing and renewal (Titus 3:5) without my awareness.

Through this experience, I realized the condition of the soul affects the accuracy of spiritual perceptions. This is especially true when it comes to emotional wounds. Damaged emotions "speak" loudly; often more loudly than God's still, small voice in our spirits.

An important point about our spiritual perception: if we want to hear God's voice clearly, we must be born again. We are given a "new spirit" when we are born from above.

Ezekiel 36:26: *Moreover, I will give you a new heart and put a **new spirit** within you; and I will remove the heart of stone from your flesh and give you a heart of flesh. (emphasis added)*

This new birth allows us to comprehend spiritual truth and see God's kingdom.

John 3:3: *Jesus answered and said to him, "Truly, truly, I say to you, unless one is born again, he cannot see the kingdom of God."*

When we are born again, the Spirit of Truth comes to live within (Rom. 8:9, 2 Tim. 1:14) and begins to sanctify our entire being, including our spiritual faculty (1 Thess. 5:23).

Even though we have communication with the Holy Spirit, it does not necessarily translate into a personal connection with Him. Similarly, we may clearly hear someone's voice on a telephone and exchange information but never personally relate with them.

If communication does not lead us to communion with God, we are limited to information only.

Information from God or perceived from spirit realm does not necessarily lead to an emotional/ heart connection or transformation

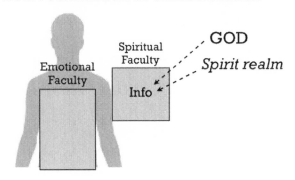

Now, this does not mean that spiritual information is of no value; it is important. God leads and helps us by communicating information and gives us knowledge and wisdom to encourage us and build up others (1 Cor. 12:7-8). But communicating and communing with God are not the same. Information alone does not transform our souls. Transformation comes when we "behold the Lord," which means we experience the excellency, beauty, and perfections of His person.

2 Corinthians 3:18: *But we all, with unveiled face, **beholding as in a mirror the glory of the Lord, are***

being transformed *into the same image from glory to glory, just as from the Lord, the Spirit. (emphasis added)*

Job learned this lesson after experiencing genuine communion with God. When Job's inner eyes opened and he beheld God, his response was, "My ears had heard of you but now my eyes have seen you. Therefore, I despise myself and repent in dust and ashes" (Job 42:5-6, NIV). Communion with God, a heart attachment to God, changes everything.

Beholding is not just a spiritual perception of God; it is also an emotional connection, Bride to Bridegroom. Our emotions are restored (Ps. 23:3; 2 Cor. 4:16; Col. 3:10), and our minds are renewed (Rom.12:1-2; Eph. 4:23) through this personal contact with the Lord Jesus.

Knowing God in this person-to-person way grounds us in truth and protects us from deception.

Communion with God Person-to-person

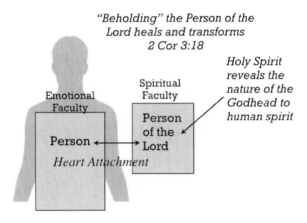

Ephesians 4:13-14: ...until we all attain to the unity of the faith, and of the knowledge [epignósis-experiential, participatory knowledge] of the Son of God, to a mature man, to the measure of the stature which belongs to the fullness of Christ. As a result, we are no longer to be children, tossed here and there by waves and carried about by every wind of doctrine, by the trickery of men, by craftiness in deceitful scheming (emphasis, brackets added)

Overuse of the Emotion Faculty

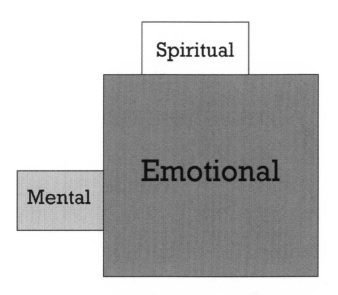

While the emotional faculty is central to our relationships with God and others, it can also be overused. Some people believe whatever feels good is right, and anything that feels bad is false. It reminds me of the lyrics to a song: "How can it be wrong if it feels so right." But when we use feelings alone to determine right from wrong and truth from lies, we are going to be misled. Even feelings of love are to be tethered, not flowing every which way. The Apostle Paul admonishes the Philippians to love with "knowledge" and "discernment."

Philippians 1:9: *And this I pray, that **your love** may abound still more and more in real **knowledge***

33

[epignósis- experiential, participatory knowledge] and all **discernment** *(emphasis, brackets added)*

When our hearts are attached to Christ and we have epignósis knowledge, we love with discernment. Experiencing God and tasting of His nature gives us a divine understanding of love and how it should be expressed. It's like having an internal database informing us as to what genuine love looks like and how feelings of love are to be administered with pure and holy boundaries. Experiencing God gives us more love for Him and others, a love that "abounds." And we will have within us a Godly perspective, a grounding, for our feelings.

Our feelings also need the balance of the other faculties. Let's say, for instance, someone is fearful that a criminal is lurking outside their home. But then they mentally recall the doors are locked and the alarm system is armed. God also gives them a spiritual sense that He is protecting them. So, the irrational feelings subside because the other faculties have given a helping hand.

However, if a person has been traumatized by a violent crime, these feelings are not so easily quieted. Wounded emotions are particularly misleading when it comes to reading situations, people, and God. Damage in the emotional faculty spills over into the other faculties and distorts perceptions, which is why it's so critical to have our emotions restored by a heart attachment to God.

Some personality types are keenly aware of their emotions and are naturally empathetic. This emotional connectedness can be a blessing and a curse. On the positive side, these abilities are conducive to relationships. But "feeler" types can find it difficult to be objective and anchored in truth because their feelings are often the loudest voice in the room. And because feelings are so important to them, making sure nobody's feelings get hurt is first and foremost. When feeling good and making others feel good is the supreme goal of life, feelings become an idol.

A feeler type can also be intensely introspective, often taking their emotional "pulse" and over-analyzing their feelings. Better for them to take a deep breath, look up, and let God do the searching of their heart.

Psalm 139:23: *Search me, O God, and know my heart; Try me and know my anxious thoughts*

My wife Jean is a feeler personality type with a high degree of emotional intelligence. I can honestly say I've never met anyone as in touch with their emotional world as she is.

Early in our marriage, Jean said confidently, "My emotions are part of my discernment." At first, this seemed a contradiction of terms to me. How could emotions discern anything? But over time, I came to realize she was onto a profound truth. The emotional faculty tells us things that other faculties do not.

However, Jean found that her emotions were not always a good barometer of truth. Just before becoming a Christian, she sensed God asking her a question: "Because you feel something, does that make it true?"

Feelers have another unique characteristic: they tend to have greater sensitivity to the sensations in their physical bodies. Awareness of emotions and the body seem to go together for these folks.

This connectedness to their body is helpful at times, but it can also lead them astray. Because they're highly aware of physical sensations, they often assume the worst. They may wrongly believe muscle tension is cancer, a headache is a brain tumor, or indigestion is an ulcer.

Keeping the emotional and physical sensations in a proper perspective can be difficult when the feelings of the soul and body are so strong.

Generally speaking, emotions are used best as a thermometer rather than a compass. They tell us what's going on inside, not what to do. We need the mental and spiritual faculties to stake out a course of action.

There can also be an over-emphasis on feelings as it relates to spiritual experiences. For some, the intensity of emotions becomes the gauge by which they judge the authenticity of a spiritual experience.

But profound experiences with God can be without intense feelings. St. John of the Cross, in his classic book Dark Night of the Soul, talks about seasons when the Christian can't feel God. His book is all about the things that happen as God takes us through the "dark night," a period of time when we feel detached from Him. St. John points out that God uses these times to: purify our devotion, give us wisdom, strip us of our old man and clothe us with the new man, renew our affections, purge us so that He might illuminate our souls, humble us so that He might exalt us, and increase our desire for Him.[4]

Amazingly, all these things are being worked in and out of our soul at a time when God feels detached and distant. In reality, when God puts us in the dark night of the soul, it can be a time when our heart attachment to Him is strengthened.

Isaiah 26:9: At night my soul longs for You; Indeed, my spirit within me seeks You diligently; For when the earth experiences Your judgments, the inhabitants of the world learn righteousness. (emphasis added)

Case Study: "The Compassionate Woman"

Daisy has a deep sense of compassion and a unique ability to find solutions to practical needs. During her childhood, she came alongside classmates with no friends and stood up to bullies. She instinctively had just the right words when a person felt down and out.

Because Daisy has the gift of compassion, she also values compassion more than any other gift. Giving and receiving compassion is her love language.

Daisy's father is a tough foreman who doesn't give her the kindness that she desperately craves. In fact, he views soft-heartedness as a sign of weakness. Unfortunately, this is exactly the opposite of what Daisy needs; her heart is pained as her dad's harsh tone pounds like a hammer into her tender heart.

She knows much of her father's harsh treatment is due to his heavy drinking, but she still feels it is somehow her fault he mistreats her. In the back of her mind, she hears: "Daisy, if you had value, your Dad would treat you with kindness and compassion."

Daisy's mind goes into crisis mode and comes up with a solution: *I'll give compassion so others will treat me compassionately and I will feel valuable*. Eventually, after Daisy has put her trust in this solution, a defense mechanism, a "mindset," forms in her thinking. This mindset drives her to be compassionate to everyone all the time with the hope of receiving the compassion she needs in return.

When Daisy leaves home, her problems continue. More than anything, she longs for a man who is kind and empathetic, but she seems to attract the complete opposite: harsh men who disregard and take advantage of her. She pours out compassion, money, resources, and time, but the men in her life continue to treat her with contempt.

After each failure, she dusts herself off and starts anew, thinking it was somehow her lack of compassion and giving that ultimately caused the problems. She resolves to give more compassion, so the same cycle continues over and over again.

One day, a Christian friend gently confronts Daisy, pointing out that there may be some issues from her past affecting her views. It's as if someone has turned the lights on in a dark room. She suddenly realizes that much of what she does in her life is based on a faulty mindset established in childhood.

Daisy feels the need to draw closer to God. As she seeks God and spends time with Him, the Holy Spirit begins the process of healing her wounded heart. For the first time, she understands that her worth comes from God and not from how much compassion she gives or receives. Several father figures also show her kindness, causing her life to shift dramatically.

As her spiritual life deepens, she realizes that she has to hold back on some of her compassion. In the past, she poured herself out in every situation and to every person.

Daisy also realizes that she needs to use her mental and spiritual faculties alongside her emotional faculty. When making decisions as to how to give compassion, she takes time to think things through and be more objective. Studying and memorizing Scripture becomes a way of life and gives her greater mental knowledge of the Word of God. This provides boundaries for her feelings. When her emotions tell her something, she takes a step back and thinks about what God's Word says.

She also learns to use her spiritual faculty and listen to the Holy Spirit's promptings, which helps her to direct her compassion. Daisy finds that when she takes time to sense what the Spirit is saying, He guides her in knowing when, how, and to whom she should give compassion.

As Daisy's heart attachment to God strengthens and her emotions are healed, the mindset which drove her to give compassion without boundaries begins to give way. She finds that the pressure to give under compulsion (2 Cor. 9:7) is no longer a temptation.

There is also something else going on in the unseen realm. Daisy now believes her value is intrinsic, and it doesn't require her giving compassion. People unconsciously pick up on this belief system and no longer take advantage of her.

CHAPTER TWO

THE EMOTIONAL FACULTY'S ATTRIBUTES

Many people are unaware that the emotional part of their being is influencing their thoughts and behaviors.

The emotional faculty would be equivalent to what the Bible calls the "heart." It is the central part of our being, and you could say, it's where we really live.

> **Proverbs 4:23:** *Above all else, guard your heart, for **everything you do flows from it**. (NIV - emphasis added)*

We all feel emotions like joy, sadness, love, and hate. But we also feel our experiences, sense of self, maturity, relationships, beliefs, values, and desires

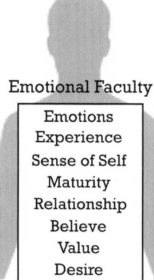

Emotional Faculty

Emotions
Experience
Sense of Self
Maturity
Relationship
Believe
Value
Desire

To a large extent, the depth of relationship we experience depends on how much we open the doors to this faculty so there can be an inward and outward flow. Allowing God full access into this part of our being allows us to experience Him most deeply.

Affections and the Will

What we are attached to from the heart ultimately determines the direction of our lives. Our spiritual conversion and ongoing walk with God is a heart-driven relationship, more than a mental determination to follow precepts. We judge the facts of the gospel to be true with our minds, but then we move on to a felt love, an attached love, a cleaving love, a love directed toward the person of God. It is with the emotional faculty that we make a marriage-like commitment to God.

Some Christians say with great assurance, "My faith in God is not based on emotions." Indeed, our faith is not based entirely on emotions. We may not feel God on a given day, and yet He is still with us. At times, we may not feel like Jesus resurrected from the dead, but it's still a historical fact. And other times we don't feel like God loves us, yet He does.

But we can't take emotions out of the mix; they play an important role in our relationships. With the emotional faculty, we choose to love God and pursue Him. Our affections, values, and desires for God flow from this faculty, so our wills are largely emotion-driven.

Jonathan Edwards, an 18th-century theologian and revivalist, was one of the great thinkers in American history. Although he was an intellectual, he saw the integral role the emotions played in the spiritual life. He used the word "affections" as we use the word "emotions" today.

Edwards believed an emotional connection with God was an absolute necessity. One could not be converted or follow God without the emotions, without a heart "inflamed" toward Him.[5] In his book, Religious Affections, Edwards stresses the critical role of our emotions:

> ...worldly affections are very much the spring of men's motion and action; so in religious matters, the spring of their actions is very much religious affection: he that has doctrinal knowledge and speculation only, without affection, never is engaged in the business of religion.[6]

43

Edwards saw the will, or "inclination," as flowing from the emotions. So we make an emotional decision to either "cleave" to and "seek" something, or to be "averse" to it and "oppose" it.7 Part of having a heart attachment to God is that we have affections for Him; we desire and love Him and find joy in His glorious nature.

The choice to attach to or turn away from God is an operation of the emotional faculty. Thus, the will has more to do with an emotional inclination than with mental decisions. Our feet go in the direction that our affections are pointed. We will pursue what we love and value. Whatever fascinates, captivates, and attracts us will be the object of our affections.

When we love God, we move toward Him. It's love that causes us to sacrifice for Him, search Him out, and attach to Him. In Matthew 13, Jesus tells a parable of a man who joyfully sells all that he has to pursue the "pearl of great value," which is the Lord Himself (Matt.13:44-46). If God is the treasure of our hearts, we will seek Him. Because we value Him, we will gladly give up things of lesser value to pursue God.

Jesus also said when we love something, we "serve" it:

Luke 16:13: *"No servant can serve two masters; for either he will hate the one and love the other, or else he will be devoted to one and despise the other. You cannot serve God and wealth."*

Many Christians believe all they need to do is be obedient to God and follow His principles. But it is because we love God that we obey Him.

John 14:23-24: *Jesus answered and said to him,* ***"If anyone loves Me, he will keep My word;*** *and My Father will love him, and We will come to him and make*

44

Our abode with him. **He who does not love Me does not keep My words;** *and the word which you hear is not Mine, but the Father's who sent Me. (emphasis added)*

Heart affections are not only necessary for conversion but also for our ongoing relationship with God. Some Christians look back on that special day when they trusted Jesus for their salvation. Much like a wedding, they had a profoundly moving experience with heartfelt commitment, joy, hope, and a fresh start. But when the wedding and honeymoon are over, they're no longer captivated by the Lord. Because they don't have their affections set on Him in an ongoing relationship, they don't grow in the heart knowledge of Him. And this lack of experiential knowledge of the Lord stunts their spiritual growth.

God provides us grace to grow in love for Him. The Holy Spirit helps us to love God and grow in a more intimate knowledge of His nature.

2 Peter 3:18: *but grow in the grace and knowledge of our Lord and Savior Jesus Christ. To Him be the glory, both now and to the day of eternity. Amen.*

It's noteworthy that God's first commandment is a directive to do something with our emotions; with our heart.

Deuteronomy 6:5: *You shall love the LORD your God* **with all your heart** *and with all your soul and with all your might. (emphasis added)*

God commands us to love Him first because a relationship is His first priority. And a relationship with Him is key to everything. But relationship requires our affections, even if they are feeble at times. It's no wonder that throughout history, God has sought the devotion of people and why He warns us of the danger of loving other things.

Solomon, the wisest man who ever lived, wrote the book of Proverbs, an instruction book for living a righteous, blessed, and full life. But he did not follow these principles and turned from God.

How could this possibly happen to someone who clearly understood Godly principles? Solomon had intellectual wisdom and understanding, but his heart was not "wholly devoted" to God. His love for his wives drew his heart away from God (1 Kings 11:1-4).

I knew a woman years ago who found herself having to make an all-important decision of the heart. At the time, we were part of a thriving Christian fellowship, and this young lady was right in the middle of everything. By every appearance, she was dedicated and dutiful in all her Christian activities.

One day, I had an impression from the Holy Spirit that she had come to a crossroads in her life. She was contemplating whether she wanted God. At first, I thought my spiritual perception could not possibly be right because she was active in the fellowship and seemed so committed to God. Yet, the Lord seemed to be telling me, "She is deciding if she wants Me." Much to my surprise, when I communicated my spiritual insight to her, she agreed it was true. Interestingly, she didn't appear to have any intellectual roadblocks but had come to a fork in the road where she was choosing to love or not to love God.

Sadly, in the months that followed, it became clear that she chose not to walk with the Lord. Edwards would say her affections were not set on God. Her heart, the center of her being, was simply not in it. Because God was not the treasure of her life, she would not make Him the focus of her affections, and therefore would not follow Him.

46

Jesus said:

Matthew 6:21: *for where your **treasure** is, there your **heart** will be also. (emphasis added)*

Some people with a more intellectual bent might argue they aren't wired for an emotional connection to people, let alone God. It's true that some types have more aptitude for emotional connection. But all of us are made in the image of a relational, trinitarian God, which means we all need a heart-to-heart, emotional relationship with God.

Our affections need to be set on God, or they will wander somewhere else. We will direct our love toward something or someone – this is inescapable; it's the way the emotional faculty operates. If our thirst isn't quenched in Jesus, our souls will remain parched, and we will look for a drink elsewhere.

John 4:13-14: *Jesus answered and said to her, "Everyone who drinks of this water will thirst again; but whoever drinks of the water that I will give him shall never thirst; but the water that I will give him will become in him a well of water springing up to eternal life."*

Knowledge through Experience

Now let's look at the epistemology of the emotional faculty: how it knows what it knows. This faculty comes to knowledge by experience. It feels experiences, primarily through relationships.

How does the mind differ from the emotions? The mental faculty acquires knowledge by reading about going to Italy, whereas the emotional faculty gains knowledge by actually traveling to Italy and having felt experiences. When it comes to emotional knowledge, you might say it's about being there.

The incarnation is an example of God stepping into our world and being with us. Jesus chose to come into our midst and become a man. Scripture tells us that He deeply understands us because he felt our struggles.

> *Hebrew 4:15: For we have not an high priest which cannot be **touched with the feeling of our infirmities**; but was in all points tempted like as we are, yet without sin. (KJV - emphasis added)*

Experiences perfected the Son of God. He went through temptations, sufferings, and trials. The Godhead's plan was for Jesus to come into the human experience, not merely to observe it. Amazing!

> *Hebrews 5:8-9: Although He was a Son, He **learned obedience** from the things which He suffered. And having been **made perfect, He became** to all those who obey Him the source of eternal salvation (emphasis added)*

The emotional faculty is an experiential organ. Through it, we feel experiences, not just emotions. We may have a profound experience but not be emotional about that experience. A child sitting on a parent's lap can have an experience and receive an impartation but not have any particular emotion accompanying it.

Growing in experiential knowledge of God does not require a person to be highly emotional. A person who is by nature more of a thinker doesn't have to become a feeler, but they do need to become a more experiential person.

The emotional faculty is also a receptor; it absorbs experiences. Experiences are a kind of information taken in by this faculty. Much like the mind stores and remembers observations, the emotional faculty stores and remembers experiences.

The movie *Good Will Hunting* highlights this kind of knowledge when the psychiatrist (played by Robin Williams) counsels a young genius (played by Matt Damon). The wise counselor is not intimidated by the boy genius's arrogance and head knowledge. He's confident his life experiences have given him a much deeper kind of knowledge:

> *You're just a kid. You don't have the faintest idea what you are talking about. You've never been out of Boston. If I asked you about art, you would probably give me the skinny on every art book ever written...Michelangelo...but, I bet you can't tell me what it smells like in the Sistine Chapel. You have never stood there and looked at that beautiful ceiling...If I ask you about war, you would probably throw Shakespeare at me: "Once more unto the breach, dear friends." But you have never been near one. You've never held your best friend's head in your lap and watched him gasp his last breath looking to you for help. You're an orphan, right? Do you think I know the first thing about how hard your life has been, how you feel, who you are, because I read Oliver Twist?*

The emotional faculty is particularly attuned to experiences of a personal kind because it has a relational component. So, the primary way that it receives impartations is through relational experiences.

You can see why it's vital to experience God in a personal way. If we don't meet God relationally, we don't grow in emotional knowledge.

The Amplified Bible translation captures the Apostle Paul's emphasis on experiential knowledge in his letter to the Ephesians:

> **Ephesians 3:19:** *and [that you may come] to know [practically, through personal experience] the love of Christ which far surpasses [mere] knowledge [without experience], that you may be filled up [throughout your being] to all the fullness of God [so that you may have the richest experience of God's presence in your lives, completely filled and flooded with God Himself]. (AMP)*

Paul uses different Greek words to refer to different types of knowledge. He uses gnósis for mental knowledge[8] and ginóskó to describe experiential and first-hand knowing.

So, Paul is saying in Ephesians 3:19 that *experientially* knowing (ginóskó) God surpasses *intellectual* knowledge (gnósis) of God.

But Paul also brings in the Greek word epignósis, which takes experiential knowledge a step further. Epignósis is experiential and flows from two persons becoming one with each other. It's the fullest, most precise, and most intimate kind of knowledge.[9]

Paul urges us on toward this kind of knowledge. He continually prays that we would move on to a bridal type of love, where we become one with the Lord.

> **Ephesians 1:17:** *I keep asking that the God of our Lord Jesus Christ, the glorious Father, may give you the Spirit of wisdom and revelation, **so that you may know [epignósis-experiential, participatory knowledge] him better.** (NIV -emphasis, brackets added)*

Trusting, loving, and setting our affections on God are ways we are interactive in knowing Him. When we love God and set our affections on Him, He gives us knowledge of Himself. He shares Himself with us within the bond of loving communion.

Over the centuries, people have seen God's wonders in Creation and had a general revelation of Him. Others have come into closer contact with God and sensed His glorious presence in some way. But few have come unto the sacred ground of participatory knowledge of God, where they experience oneness with their Bridegroom.

Sense of Self

Our sense of self, or how we feel about ourselves, is another part of the emotional faculty. This sense of personhood has a significant influence on how we conduct our lives. Like a strong undercurrent, it can take us off in a direction or stop us cold in our tracks. It also affects our relationships.

Many people have an idea of what they would like to do with their lives and maybe have a detailed vocational plan. But when they try to execute this plan, they get stuck because their sense of self won't allow them to move forward.

Let's say someone is going through the process of growing a garden. To accomplish this, a person goes through the process of becoming a gardener. They must take on the *identity* of a gardener.

This person begins by envisioning the garden: what they will plant, where to dig up the soil, what fertilizer they need, etc. At this point, they are using the creative, "big-picture" function of the right brain to conceptualize the garden and haven't yet used their more detail-oriented left brain to implement their ideas. But then the sense of self comes into play: how they feel about themselves as a gardener. If they feel competent and worthy to be a gardener, there's a smooth transition to their left brain where they can actually do the gardening.

Negative experiences may influence their sense of self. Perhaps they were shamed while trying to put their creative ideas into practice in the past, which damaged their sense of self. So, now they fear implementing their gardening ideas.

The sense of self effectively becomes the bridge from the conceptual part of gardening to the actual gardening.

Sense of self is a bridge from right brain to left brain

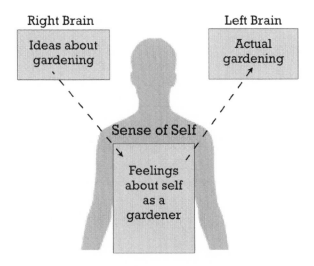

Issues related to the sense of self, identity issues, are often the barriers to people walking out their vision.

In the early years of my flying career, I had a check ride, which is a test pilots take periodically for certification. This particular test had my stomach in knots. Any pilot will tell you these tests are stressful; it's just part of being a professional pilot. But this check ride really shook me up. After pondering the experience for some time, I realized that I was terrified of failing. This may sound shocking, but I was honestly more afraid of failing a test in an airplane than crashing and dying in an airplane. My sense of self was on the line with this test, and, to me, failing meant I was a failure as a person.

Our sense of self is always in play when we start down a path. How we feel about ourselves really does matter. A healthy sense of self enables us to walk down a road and complete things, while an unhealthy sense of self is an emotional barrier to our goals.

Of course, this brings up the question, what do we do with a damaged sense of self? Some might say we need to be less self-oriented and more Christ-centered. That's partially true, but we can't get rid of our sense of self, or step out of our skin, as it were. Others might advocate fighting through feelings of insecurity, using the mind to overcome the emotions. There's a measure of truth here, as well. As we discussed, the mind does help stabilize emotions. But this is just coping with the issue, and the problem remains. What we need is a renewed and healthy sense of self.

You might say, "I just want to do things for God...it's not about me." But it is about you! Your sense of self goes along for the ride, whether you are pursuing a goal, working a job, or doing something for God. In fact, we really can't fulfill our calling without a healthy sense of self. A leader has mental, emotional, and intuitive abilities to lead; but because of a damaged sense of self, they may not be able to function as a leader. A distorted sense of self can cap their abilities and keep them bottled up inside. It feels too risky to step out, so they keep their leadership talents hidden.

For those who have a distorted sense of self, it's not the end of the story. If we get help from the outside, from God Himself, our sense of self can be restored.

No matter how much we try to think our way into emotional health or give ourselves an internal makeover, we end up back at the same point. Restoration of our sense of self and the emotional faculty, in general, requires God's intervention.

Relationship

Through the emotional faculty, we understand and connect to others; we feel people and God. Much like a highly sensitive antenna, this faculty is tuned into a relational frequency and is sensitive to the emotions of others. It picks up on relational issues that the other faculties do not.

One could even say the emotions are a form of discernment. Many understand the concept of spiritual discernment, but emotional discernment is a bit different. The emotional faculty is relationally discerning. For instance, it discerns emotional openness, as well as emotional distance. Or when a relational boundary is crossed, there may be a feeling that something's not quite right.

The emotional faculty is the contact point for the emotions of another person. It is the faculty by which we know another person's inner man. When we share from the emotional faculty, others may feel or experience us via their emotional faculty. "I feel" or "I desire" statements open the doors of the emotional faculty so that others can experience us. In this way, they have contact with our inner person. As I stated earlier, this was my experience when my friends asked me to share what I felt. When I revealed from my emotional faculty, I felt vulnerable and somewhat uncovered, but the payoff was an emotional connection. My friends and I both experienced relationship when I swung open the gates to my inner person.

This kind of emotional connection also can be experienced with God. Although we perceive Him through our spirit, we relate to Him through our emotional faculty. Here is where we meet God person-to-person.

Listen to the Psalmist's emotional hunger for a personal connection with God.

> **Psalm 84:2:** *My* **soul** *longed and even yearned for the courts of the LORD; My* **heart** *and my* **flesh** *sing for joy to the living God. (emphasis added)*

> **Psalm 42:2**: *My* **soul** *thirsts for God, for the living God; When shall I come and appear before God? (emphasis added)*

There are essential doctrines we need to know intellectually about God and the Christian faith, and God does reveal important information to our spirits. But there is also a knowledge that can only be grasped by connecting to God emotionally. The Apostle Paul had intellectual knowledge and a clear understanding of doctrine, but he also had a passion for relational knowledge of God. He thirsted for intimate knowledge of Christ.

> **Philippians 3:7-8:** *But whatever things were gain to me, those things I have counted as loss for the sake of Christ. More than that,* **I count all things to be loss in view of the surpassing value of knowing Christ Jesus** *my Lord, for whom I have suffered the loss of all*

things and count them but rubbish so that I may gain Christ. (emphasis added)

We see this personal dynamic in Paul's letter to the Galatian church when he speaks of Christ "being formed" in them.

Galatians 4:19: *My Children, with whom I am again in labor until Christ is formed in you*

A person formed in us: what an unusual concept! This formation is more than a download of spiritual data. Through relational encounters, we become unified with the Person of Christ, which results in the formation of His nature in us.

We cannot truly relate to God without the emotional faculty. We are connected to the Spirit of God as Christians but are not personally connected until we engage Him emotionally. Two people meeting regularly for coffee, speaking only about things like the weather or the cars they drive, will have little in the way of personal connectedness. However, incorporating the emotional faculty into the relationship allows them actually to experience and know one another.

We can have spiritual revelations from God and do things in Christ's name and still not have experiential knowledge of Him.

Matthew 7:22-23: *"Many will say to me on that day, 'Lord, Lord, did we not prophesy in your name and in your name drive out demons and in your name perform many miracles?' Then I will tell them plainly, 'I never* **knew** *[ginóskó –knew experientially] you. Away from me, you evildoers!'" (NIV -emphasis, brackets added)*

56

Believe

While there is a rational component to believing, it's with the heart that we have a personal, felt belief in the character of God. A bridal relationship with the Lord requires this kind of personal trust. We are not just trusting a concept with the mind but embracing a person (the Lord) with the heart.

There's a kind of trust where we make a mental assessment that a bridge is sturdy and won't collapse when we cross it. But there's another kind of trust in who God is that helps us to actually walk across that bridge. It is a faith in His attributes – His goodness, power, and faithfulness – as well as the confidence that God has concern and care for us; that He has affections *for us*.

> ***Zephaniah 3:17****: The LORD thy God in the midst of thee is mighty; he will save, **he will rejoice over thee** with joy; he will rest in his love, **he will joy over thee** with singing. (KJV -emphasis added)*

When we make a personal commitment and attachment *from the heart* to trust God, He supports us and gives us an emotional strength to move forward on our life journey.

> ***Romans 6:17****: But thanks be to God that though you were slaves of sin, you became obedient **from the heart** to that form of teaching to which **you were committed** (emphasis added)*

Through a heart belief in God, we experience internal security; we become unified with the "Chief Cornerstone" (Eph. 2:20) and "the Rock" (1 Cor. 10:4). Jesus's remedy for a troubled heart is to "believe in God."

John 14:1: *"Do not let your heart be troubled; believe in God, believe also in Me."*

A change truly takes place when we go beyond a mental belief about God to heart belief *in Him*. When we trust in God's character as a person, we become emotionally attached to God and we receive security and life from His nature. God gave Abram an incredible promise for trusting Him; God gave Himself as a "reward."

Genesis 15:1: *After these things the word of the LORD came unto Abram in a vision, saying, Fear not, Abram:* **I am** *thy shield,* and **thy exceeding great reward**. *(KJV - emphasis added)*

Value

In the emotional faculty, we possess values that are felt and motivate us from the heart. Some values we choose, and other values God determines for us.

When we direct our heart affections toward something or someone, we are choosing our values. We may embrace values such as God, family, community, effectiveness, excellence, generosity, success, or creativity.

God also gives us a value for our strengths. He sovereignly weaves this value into our unique personalities, so we naturally value our strengths and what we are called to do in life.

Someone with a God-given gift for managing people has mental and spiritual abilities to manage along with an emotional value for management.

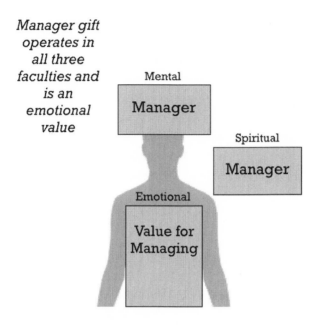

Manager gift operates in all three faculties and is an emotional value

The manager naturally thinks, senses, and values management. God not only gives them abilities but also a heart-motivation to manage. This built-in emotional value makes them feel that management is important and what the world needs more than anything else.

So, the business manager will feel that managing is the key to running a successful company. If an employee is underperforming or something isn't working, efficient management will be their answer.

Another person working in the same company sees things differently because they have different strengths and values. A trainer values the dissemination of information. Acquiring knowledge is the essential thing, and if the business is failing, it's because the employees haven't received proper training.

An employee in the human resources department, whose strength is compassion, sees it in yet another way. In this person's view, making employees feel accepted and part of the corporate family is what is most important.

So, each person has emotional values that correspond with their mental and spiritual abilities. The manager values managing, the trainer values training, and the compassionate person values compassion. God hard-wires these values into their emotional faculties to motivate and propel their unique gifts and talents.

Desire

Another attribute of the emotional faculty is *desire*. Desire is felt; we feel hope, longing, and fulfillment.

Desire is meant to lead us down the path that God destined for us. He has made our souls thirsty and hungry so that we might be filled.

Psalm 107:9: For He has satisfied the thirsty soul, and the hungry soul He has filled with what is good.

Our desire is God's way of propelling us toward Him and His purposes. This doesn't mean every desire is from God. There is a contingency: If we "delight in God" and have Him as our first love, then our desires will align with His.

Psalm 37:4: Delight yourself in the LORD; And He will give you the desires of your heart.

Psalm 145:19: He will fulfill the desire of those who fear Him; He will also hear their cry and will save them.

Desire has two distinct components: *longing* and *fulfillment.* Longing is forward-looking, and fulfillment takes place in the present when a desire is "realized."

Proverbs 13:19a: Desire realized is sweet to the soul.

Either of these components of desire – longing or fulfillment – can be inactive. Some find it difficult to want for anything; the longing part of them is inactive. Others are wounded in their desire, so longing is painful, and they avoid it altogether.

But we need to have hope; it's the spark plug for the engine of our soul. Hope gets us up and moving and is one of God's primary methods of aligning us with His purposes.

Desire leads us to seek out what we need. Like hunger drives us to find nourishment for our physical bodies, we crave things that will satisfy the appetites of our souls.

Psalm 63:5: My soul is satisfied as with marrow and fatness, and my mouth offers praises with joyful lips.

Psalm 107:9: For He has satisfied the thirsty soul, and the hungry soul He has filled with what is good.

Some people have a well-developed vision for their life. They understand what they must do and have taken steps toward making their dream a reality. The longing part of their desire is up and running, and the future looks bright. But then maybe their vision doesn't come to pass. Or at least it doesn't come to pass in the way they expected, so they struggle with their unfulfilled desires. The Bible says we become "heartsick" when our desire is unrealized or "deferred."

Proverbs 13:12: *Hope deferred makes the heart sick, but desire fulfilled is a tree of life.*

Notice that the fulfillment of a desire is the tree of life. Obviously, God has made fulfillment a source of life and something to be enjoyed. It is life-giving and satisfying to the taste buds of our souls.

For most of us, there's a time when our vision seems to get temporarily stuck in the mud. This in-between time can be a real endurance test, requiring trust in God and His timing. We don't want to give up our hope at this stage or shut down our desire.

Sometimes, however, we are expecting too much from earthly dreams. We can't expect the arrival of a spouse, job, or house to fulfill our ultimate longings.

All earthly desires are but streams, but God is the ocean

~ Jonathan Edwards

God required Abraham to put Isaac on the altar (Gen. 22:2). How difficult it must have been to offer up Issac, the fulfillment of Abraham's desire. But God would not allow Isaac to be his highest hope. We may have to, as Abraham did, put our vision on the altar and attach ourselves to the "God of hope."

Roman 15:13: *Now may the God of hope fill you with all joy and peace in believing, so that you will abound in hope by the power of the Holy Spirit.*

Relationship with God fulfills our deepest longings for affection, security, and hope. It also creates in us a desire for His will. We delight in God, finding fulfillment in the excellencies of His character, and then we quite naturally want to do things for Him. We work out what God works in.

> **Philippians 2:12-13:** *So then, my beloved, just as you have always obeyed, not as in my presence only, but now much more in my absence, **work out** your salvation with fear and trembling; for it is God who is at **work in** you, both to will and to work for His good pleasure. (emphasis added)*

To be a player in the game of life we need hope. If we take our longings out of the equation, we are removing ourselves from the playing field. Our desire needs to be alive and active. God can awaken a desire in us for Himself, as well as a longing to fulfill His purposes.

There's a solid hope for the future when Christians realize they are God's precious possession. God looks at the Church as His "inheritance," those who will fulfill His purposes on this earth. We also can look forward to eternal life, a glorious future in heaven, and a place in God's eternal kingdom.

> **Ephesians 1:18:** *I pray that the eyes of your heart may be enlightened, so that you will know what is **the hope of His calling, what are the riches of the glory of His inheritance in the saints,** (emphasis added)*

Desire is powerful; it inspires us to pursue a vision, and we enjoy a wonderful feeling of fulfillment upon reaching a goal. Most importantly, desire motivates us to seek the One who satisfies our deepest longings.

Case Study: "The Righteous Man"

Jim has a high value for righteousness, apparent even as a young boy. He views things as either right or wrong, black or white. When his parents ask him why he no longer spends time with a neighbor boy, he responds with, "He swears a lot and tells too many lies."

Because Jim's drive for righteousness is so strong, he rarely needs to be disciplined by his parents. The threat of peer pressure is nonexistent as his inner compass always points him directly to honesty, righteousness, and holiness.

As Jim grows older, he feels drawn to the priesthood, believing this is maybe a way to pursue a life of holiness, a theme that is continuously in the back of his mind.

But Jim has some mixed motivations for seeking such a calling. On the one hand, he desires to make a Godly stand for righteousness in the community. But Jim has serious doubts whether his holiness meets up to the standards of such a call. Secretly he hopes that becoming a priest will put to rest some of his feelings of unrighteousness and unworthiness.

Jim finds himself in an impossible situation. He feels the high calling to live a life of holiness, yet feels he is utterly failing to meet up to Godly standards.

A shaming message penetrates Jim's emotions: *If you don't meet up to high standards of righteousness, you are worthless.* And then a mindset develops in his thinking: *I will strive to be righteous to feel valuable.*

Being a priest seems like the perfect occupation because he can concentrate on being completely devoted, righteous, holy, and pure. So, Jim goes to seminary in preparation for a life in the cloth.

But much like Martin Luther centuries ago, Jim becomes more and more troubled by his inability to live righteously. This particular verse leaves a knot in his stomach:

Romans 3:12: They are all gone out of the way, they are together become unprofitable; there is none that doeth good, no, not one. (KJV)

As his eyes run over the text, anxiety grips him. Jim's protective mindset is in overdrive trying to keep the shame from overwhelming him. It's a catch 22. He must, according to his mindset, be perfectly righteous, but he sees in the Scriptures that this is not possible. And then the Holy Spirit leads him to a verse that forever changes Jim's life:

Romans 5:8-9: But God demonstrates His own love toward us, in that while we were yet sinners, Christ died for us. Much more then, having now been justified by His blood, we shall be saved from the wrath of God through Him.

For the first time in his life, Jim comes to understand that he cannot by his works achieve right standing before God. It must be received by faith in Christ's righteousness, as seen in Paul's letter to the Philippians:

Philippians 3:9: ...and may be found in Him, not having a righteousness of my own derived from the Law, but that which is through faith in Christ, the righteousness which comes from God on the basis of faith.

65

A Holy Spirit conviction comes over him as he senses the need to completely trust Christ's atoning sacrifice to be right with God. He finally realizes that because God reached out to him "while he was a sinner" (Rom. 5:8) his performance was never the reason that God loved him. Jim always had infinite value to God.

As he prays in his seminary room, he suddenly has a sense of righteousness that is unrelated to his performance. He understands he is saved from God's wrath through Jesus. It feels like the weight of the world has been taken off his back. He takes comfort in Paul's words that he has a righteousness that is "not his own."

But he is not out of the woods yet because his emotional faculty contradicts the other faculties. He does not "know" truth in his emotions, and the old voice of shame continues to tell him that he needs to obtain righteousness through works. The protective mindset he had before his conversion is still in place because his emotions have not been restored.

So, Jim finds it difficult to keep the horse before the cart, sometimes falling into a legalistic approach to personal holiness, rather than the empowerment of the Holy Spirit. Verses like 1 Peter 1:16 are hard for him to digest.

1 Peter 1:16: ...because it is written, "YOU SHALL BE HOLY, FOR I AM HOLY."

But, as Jim experiences God's fatherly nature, he begins to emotionally understand that he has intrinsic value. He no longer fears God will discard him for the slightest misstep. As Jim encounters God's loving kindness and grace in personal, intimate ways, the tormenting fear he previously felt about not being "good enough" is replaced with a healthy fear of the Lord.

CHAPTER THREE

THE EMOTIONAL FACULTY'S

OPERATIONS

Emotional Impartations

Our emotional faculty receives impartations from people and God. An emotional impartation is a transference of emotional knowledge from one person to another.

Impartations can come through verbal communication, but they can come by other means as well. We can receive an impartation by being in someone's presence. Impartations have more to do with a person giving something of their nature to another person, one heart to another heart. And to a large extent, a person can only provide the impartations they have already received.

Remember, communicating and communing with God is not the same. Communication is the transfer of information, but communion is the transfer of nature.

When we experience God, He imparts His nature into ours. For example, when we experience God's love, our emotional faculty is "filled" with this particular attribute of His.

Ephesians 3:19: *...and to **know** [ginóskó – experientially know] the love of Christ, which surpasses knowledge, **that you may be filled** up to all the fullness of God. (emphasis, brackets added)*

Without impartations, there's a vacuum in our emotional faculty. This lack of emotional knowledge causes us to question ourselves; we wonder if we are loved, safe, or significant.

An impartation is not just a momentary or passing feeling, but a truth woven into the fabric of the emotional being. With this deposit comes a tangible sense of security and permanent change to the inner man.

Take the example of a young man who we will call "John." John grew up in an orphanage where there was very little love, guidance, nurturing, or identification.

Later in life, John becomes a Christian. He is amazed to read about the God of the Bible who wants to be personally involved in his life.

John has no problem mentally comprehending the fact that he is a child of God after reading the Word of God (John 1:12). The Holy Spirit also testifies to the fact that he is God's child (Rom. 8:16), so he has spiritual knowledge of sonship.

But something about the concept doesn't feel like reality. What's going on here? John lacks emotional knowledge. He didn't have the experience of being loved by his parents, so he has an emotional deficit. Because of this, it feels like God is also distant and uncaring. So, John doesn't feel like a son or experience his sonship.

Let's go back to an earlier diagram:

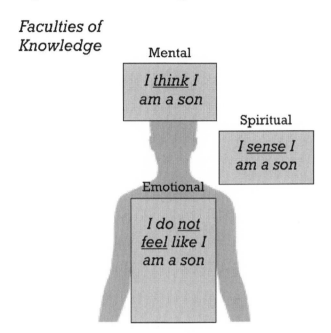

Faculties of Knowledge

Mental — *I think I am a son*

Spiritual — *I sense I am a son*

Emotional — *I do not feel like I am a son*

You can see John has mental and spiritual knowledge of sonship but is missing emotional knowledge, which comes through experience.

The emotional faculty is like a container filled with various relational experiences. These experiences stay with a person. Different aspects of security, such as guidance, affirmation, identification, and affection, become a part of a person's emotional DNA.

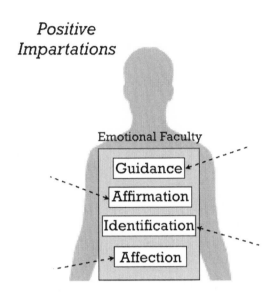

Positive Impartations

Emotional Faculty

Guidance
Affirmation
Identification
Affection

If we receive positive impartations from human relationships, we will have a greater sense of security. These kinds of impartations also make for an easier transition to a relationship with God.

But there are limits to what we can get from human impartations. God's intent has always been to impart Himself, to share His nature, so that we might be secure. If we are willing to set our focus on knowing His person, there's no limit to what He will impart into our souls.

But this requires a *living* relationship with God, where we become attached to Him. So our Christianity can't just be a ticket to heaven, a way to get blessings, or a means to reach our personal goals. It must be about knowing God personally; a seeking of God's *face*.

When a person realizes they need an emotional impartation, they invariably ask, "What must I do to get an impartation?" They often feel they have to do something or motivate God to act. Because they have an emotional deficit, they have little expectation for impartations coming their way. It's hard for them to imagine God, of His own will, would initiate a loving interaction with them. And it's difficult to understand that instead of trying to get God to move on their behalf, they need to *receive* from Him. This comes by developing a stronger heart attachment to God, by gazing on His wonderful attributes and expecting Him to be an active and involved Father.

Jesus said that life was in Him, and knowing Him would be food for our souls. But the people didn't have a framework for this sort of "eating," so they went back to something familiar.

> ***John 6:27-29****: "Do not work for the food which perishes, but for **the food which endures to eternal life**, which the Son of Man will give to you, for on Him the Father, God, has set His seal." Therefore they said to Him, "**What shall we do, so that we may work the works of God?**" Jesus answered and said to them, "This is the work of God, that you believe in Him whom He has sent." (emphasis added)*

Jesus was shifting the focus onto Himself; He is the food and drink that will impart life into our souls. Coming in contact with His nature gives sustenance to the soul.

> ***John 6:35****: Jesus said to them, "**I am the bread of life**; he who comes to Me will not hunger, and he who believes in Me will never thirst. (emphasis added)*

Emotional impartations have a profound impact on a person's soul. This is true of the non-Christian, as well. One paradox I have seen is that some non-Christians have a higher degree of emotional intelligence than Christians because of the positive impartations they have received from people.

The risen Christ is alive in the believer's spirit, but this doesn't mean they have *emotional understanding*. The born-again Christian has a new spiritual nature (2 Cor. 5:17) and has been enlightened (John 3:3) to see eternal realities. But they still may not have received emotional impartations or experienced the renewal of the mind. Renovation of the soul requires an ongoing, experiential relationship with Jesus after the initial conversion experience.

Thankfully, if we are willing to turn toward God and attach our hearts to Him, He will give us emotional impartations and align our soul with the perfect Spirit who resides within.

Colossians 3:10: *...and have put on the new self, which is **being renewed in knowledge in the image** of its Creator. (NIV - emphasis added)*

The Neutrality of the Soul

One common misconception is that the soul itself is evil, rather than what occupies it.

Some have a dualistic view, believing that the spiritual part of a person is good and the soul part is bad. But in reality, the soul is a neutral ground where good fruit develops through the Spirit of God or bad fruit grows from a "fleshly" life.

Galatians 6:8: *For the one who sows to his own flesh will from the flesh reap corruption, but the one who sows to the Spirit will from the Spirit reap eternal life.*

The soul can be tainted and, in fact, because of Adam's fall, we are born into this world with a corrupted soul. When we are born again in Christ, we receive a new nature, and the Holy Spirit goes about renewing our souls and sanctifying us.

In one sense the Christian has been "perfected," but there is also a progressive perfecting, a renewal and "sanctification" of the soul.

Hebrews 10:14: *For by one offering He **has perfected** forever those who are **being sanctified**. (NKJV - emphasis added)*

The soul is like a field, which is neither good nor bad. Within that field is good or bad soil, good or bad fruit, and weeds that take over that field. The farmer removes the bad fruit and pulls weeds so good fruit might grow. He doesn't get rid of the entire field!

Our soul is not the adversary. But rather, our enemy is the things that corrupt, damage, and "war against" our souls.

1 Peter 2:11: *Beloved, I urge you as aliens and strangers to abstain from fleshly lusts which wage war against the soul.*

The soul is likened to a "vessel." We choose to have our vessel "cleansed," "sanctified," and used for either "honor" or dishonor.

75

2 Timothy 2:21: *Therefore, if anyone cleanses himself from these things, he will be a vessel for honor, sanctified, useful to the Master, prepared for every good work.*

Some people believe whatever originates from their soul is evil. So, they might view their feelings as an evil that needs to be buried and never see the light of day. They don't process, work through, or release their emotions. And they don't take the time to figure out what their feelings are telling them.

The goal is not to stifle emotions but to be able to identify them and express them in a godly way. The Lord gives us the latitude to "be angry" but not "sin."

Ephesians 4:26: *Be ye angry, and sin not: let not the sun go down upon your wrath. (KJV)*

During my college years, when I was convinced that emotions should never be let out of the bag, I had an eye-opening experience. One of my classmates invited me to his home for dinner with his very expressive Greek family.

Honestly, when these Greeks began conversing at the dinner table, I thought I was watching the breakup of an American family. They would express a feeling, bite into some food, express a little more, take a sip of water. Every topic was fair game. My head was on a swivel, looking around the table, wondering where it was all going. After the meal was over, I was stunned, but they carried on as if nothing had happened.

Later, I realized that far from being a dysfunctional family, they had *emotional literacy*. Meaning, they were skillful at identifying and expressing their emotions and listening well as the others expressed their feelings.[10] Because this family understood how to operate in their soul, they could share themselves, connect, and be known by others.

76

The first commandment instructs us to love God "with *all* our soul":

Mark 12:30: *Love the Lord your God with all your heart and **with all your soul** and with all your mind and with all your strength. (NIV - emphasis added)*

Our individual and distinct personhood is also part of our soul. Relating to God and loving Him requires us to bring ourselves, our unique personhood, to the table to commune with Him. By *personhood*, I mean our feelings, thoughts, motivations, desires, values, wounds, fears, inspirations, and loves. All the things that make us a unique person.

Some people have difficulty relating because they have taken their personhood out of the relationship equation. It may feel safer to keep themselves out of their interactions with God and people. They may cloak this by saying something along the lines of, "Life is all about serving God and helping others." But denying our personhood keeps us from experiencing God and other people, and it prevents us from really being known. And we can't feel fully loved when we are not fully known.

Others feel unworthy to approach God, so they keep their inner selves out of their interactions with God. They may pray to God and serve God, but they don't bring their soul to Him. They're then unable to attach to God because it is with the soul that we choose to love God and have a person-to-person relationship. After removing their personhood, at best, they can only communicate with God, not commune with Him.

Our soul is precious territory that God wants to renovate. He doesn't want to annihilate our soul or our distinct personality but to transform, renew, and sanctify it. A transformed soul is a glorious thing!

Emotional Maturity

The emotional faculty can mature. There's an intangible quality, a certain *nature*, that the emotionally mature possess in their inner being. They listen well, ask questions, are empathetic and other-orientated, and at the same time have a clear sense of identity and security.

A person may *act* mature outwardly but not *be* mature inwardly. Some people are intelligent, wise, gifted, educated, socially adept, yet emotionally immature.

There is an aspect of maturity that involves an intellectual choice to act like an adult. The Apostle Paul tells us to think with maturity.

> **1 Corinthians 14:20:** *Brethren, do not be children in your thinking; yet in evil be infants,* **but in your thinking be mature**. *(emphasis added)*

But it's challenging to think and act with maturity when our inner being is not mature. In the long haul, it is emotional maturity that produces mature thinking and behaviors. It's not something we can just put on; maturity is an inner quality that gets worked into our emotional faculty.

How do we become emotionally mature? One way is through trials. Some people remain emotional adolescents well into their adulthood because they've never had to press through difficulties that strengthen their emotional muscles. Henry Cloud and John Townsend talk about the importance of experiencing life's limits in their classic book Boundaries.

> *Many out-of-control adolescents don't mature until their late thirties, when they become tired of not having a*

steady job and a place to stay. They have to hit bottom financially, and sometimes they may even have to live on the streets for a while. In time, they begin sticking with a career, saving money, and starting to grow up. They gradually begin to accept life's limits.[11]

God uses trials to develop maturity in His children.

James 1:2-4: *Consider it pure joy, my brothers and sisters, whenever you **face trials** of many kinds, because you know that the testing of your faith produces perseverance. Let perseverance finish its work **so that you may be mature** and complete, not lacking anything. (NIV - emphasis added)*

God has a hands-on approach to maturing His sons and daughters. The Holy Spirit is actively involved and applies all means to develop inward maturity in the children of God (Heb. 12:6). I have seen this play out countless times. Difficulties and struggles often mark a Christian's life because *God* sends them into a desert experience. Even Jesus was driven into the desert by the Holy Spirit.

Mark 1:12: *The Spirit immediately drove him out into the wilderness. (ESV)*

Part of making God the Lord of our lives is to humbly submit to His maturation process and not "despise" His fatherly discipline.

Proverbs 3:11-12: *My son, do not despise the LORD's discipline, and do not resent his rebuke, because the LORD disciplines those he loves, as a father the son he delights in. (NIV)*

Christians can suddenly find themselves in a divine boot camp where God puts them through stretching experiences, relational conflicts, and fiery testing. This "refining" is sent to purify and mature.

Isaiah 48:10: *"Behold, I have refined you, but not as silver; I have tested you in the furnace of affliction."*

Maturity develops not just because we experience trials but because we get to *know God* through the difficulties. In fact, knowledge of God is essential to becoming an adult Christian. As Oswald Chambers sees it, knowing God more deeply is part of the progression from a "babe" to "mature adult":

...the apostle links our maturity with the "knowledge of the Son of God" (Eph. 4:13). To know Him more fully and deeply is an essential factor in attaining maturity, and that is necessarily a progressive thing, for we are exhorted to "grow in the...knowledge of our Lord and Savior Jesus Christ" (2 Pet. 3:18). Ideally, we begin our spiritual lives as babes in Christ; then we progress through spiritual adolescence; finally we attain to a mature adult status.[12]

Chambers simplifies maturity into a "Christlikeness" that flows from intimacy with God and "seeing Jesus as He is":

What will the mature Christian be like? He will be like Christ. Spiritual maturity, expressed in the simplest terms, is – Christlikeness. We are mature only insofar as we are like Him. That concept is borne out of the fact that, when we attain full maturity at Christ's second advent, "we shall be like Him, because we shall see Him just as He is" (1 John 3:2).[13]

80

Our maturity can be measured by how well we reflect the image of Christ (Col. 3:10).

We all have both mature and immature parts of our souls. At times the adult part motivates us and other times the childish part. We progressively mature as we yield to the Holy Spirit and come to know God more intimately; as we become more like Christ.

Such was the case with the Apostle Paul. In one sense, he considered himself to be a mature Christian.

Philippians 3:15: All of us, then, who are mature should take such a view of things. And if on some point you think differently, that too God will make clear to you. (NIV -emphasis added)

But Paul also saw himself on a progressive journey to become fully mature as he "took hold" and became attached to Christ Jesus.

*Philippians 3:12: Not that I have already reached the goal or am already fully mature, but I make every effort to **take hold** of it because I also have been taken hold of by Christ Jesus. (HCSB - emphasis added)*

Peter Scazzero, in the subtitle of his excellent book *Emotionally Healthy Spirituality*, makes a profound statement: "It's impossible to be spiritually mature while remaining emotionally immature."[14]

Spiritual maturity is more than just following godly principles, knowing a lot of biblical information, or being spiritually discerning. Maturity involves the state of our inner person, our emotional faculty.

Eventually, our inner core will show itself, as Scazzero points out when describing his journey as a pastor of a large, successful

81

church. He came to a point in his personal and church life when he says the "cracks" in his inner foundation began to show:

I had ignored the "emotional component"' in my seeking of God for seventeen years. The spiritual-discipleship approaches of the churches and ministries that had shaped me did not have the language, theology, or training to help me in this area. It didn't matter how many books I read or seminars I attended in the other areas: physical, social, intellectual, spiritual. It didn't matter how many years passed, whether seventeen or another thirty. I would remain an emotional infant until this was exposed and transformed through Jesus Christ. The spiritual foundation upon which I had built my life (and had taught others) was cracked.15

Ironically, the very things that people are doing that may look mature outwardly can keep them from gaining maturity within. Some people try to protect themselves emotionally by doing things that appear spiritual and mature, essentially putting on a false self. But this prevents them from growing emotionally and spiritually.

Emotional trauma can also stunt our emotional maturity. Wounding and deficits make us want to cover our emotions and detach from God, which stops the maturation process.

We can't help but be changed when we attach to the One who is secure, stable, and able to deliver. When God shares His fatherly nature with us, it produces mature thoughts, motivations, and behaviors.

A Parent's Heart

The Apostle Paul had a parental heart. We can see the relational nature of his ministry in his letters to the early churches. He refers to himself as a "father" (1 Cor. 4:15), and at one point says he cared for the believers like a "nursing mother caring for her children" (1 Thess. 2:7). He also referred to the letters' recipients as his "children" (Gal.4:19; 1 Cor. 4:14).

Paul wasn't just a minister of Christian doctrine but was a *father* in the faith to the churches he served. He related with others and imparted something of himself into them.

Deborah was a judge and prophetess in Israel who gave wise counsel, prophetic utterances, and military directives. But Deborah chose to call herself a *mother* and had a parental *heart* for the people she led.

> *Judges 5:7: "The peasantry ceased, they ceased in Israel, until I, Deborah, arose, until I arose, **a mother in Israel**. (emphasis added)*

> *Judges 5:9: "**My heart goes out** to the commanders of Israel, the volunteers among the people; Bless the LORD! (emphasis added)*

People grasp things with greater depth and clarity when a message is delivered in the context of a relationship and with the nature of Christ. "Speaking the truth in love" makes all the difference.

> *Ephesians 4:15: ...but speaking the truth in love, we are to grow up in all aspects into Him who is the head, even Christ.*

God also imparts truth into us through relationship. Notice how Scripture says "grace and peace" are multiplied through epignósis knowledge, an experiential and person-to-person knowledge.

2 Peter 1:2: *Grace and peace be multiplied to you in the knowledge [epignósis- experiential, participatory knowledge] of God and of Jesus our Lord. (brackets added)*

The Apostle Paul was a strict follower of Judaism and knew its doctrine inside and out. But then Paul met Jesus. His dramatic conversion to Christianity wasn't just a shift in doctrine (although it was that). He actually met Jesus Christ. Paul didn't become a Christian because he "figured it out," but because Jesus revealed himself to Paul.

Galatians 1:16: *...to reveal His Son in me so that I might preach Him among the Gentiles, I did not immediately consult with flesh and blood.*

Paul evaluated all the things that made him feel righteous, knowledgeable, and special (Phil. 3:4-6) in the past; and deemed them valueless compared to knowing Jesus.

Philippians 3:8: *More than that, **I count all things to be loss in view of the surpassing value of knowing Christ Jesus my Lord**, for whom I have suffered the loss of all things, and count them but rubbish so that I may gain Christ (emphasis added)*

There is a vital part of growth and maturity that comes through a relational impartation, both from people and God. And it's much more challenging to be a father or mother to others if we've not been parented well. To a large degree, we can only give what we have received.

Emotional maturity is vital because it affects our ability to be fathers and mothers to the next generation. When we interact with others, we don't just pass on information to them. We also share with them our inner qualities and character. You could say, we give them a part of ourselves; a part of who we are. Actual parenting has a somewhat intangible quality. It is not so much about the how of parenting, but the who of parenting. There is a state of being a father or mother, which then affects the state of being of their children. I have marveled at men and women who exude a parental nature that went far beyond merely transferring intellectual knowledge or wisdom. They knew what parenting was from an emotional perspective because they had experienced a parent's impartation and could then impart what they had received to others.

Impartations can also happen in the context of spiritual parenting. I attended a church where there were two pastors. One was an excellent teacher who brought forth profound truths. Every Sunday, I looked forward to his amazing teachings. But during the week, in his daily interactions with people, he lacked the nature of a father. In fact, he seemed to be in competition with people and needed them to know that he was "in charge." Often his behavior was more like an adolescent than an adult.

The other pastor's sermons were not particularly memorable, and his demeanor was less refined. But he had that rare fatherly quality which allowed others to feel his care tangibly. Deep down, they knew he was looking out for them and truly wanted them to succeed, something fathers desire for their children. It wasn't just his words that impacted people, but his fatherly nature. The maturity he possessed was there for a reason: his simple, profound relationship with his Heavenly Father.

85

Fathers have been fathered. Fathering can happen through natural fathers but, ultimately, divine fathering is most impactful. In this verse, the Apostle John says that fathers have come to "know God" experientially.

> *1 John 2:12-13: I am writing to you, little children, because your sins have been forgiven you for His name's sake. I am writing to you, **fathers, because you know [ginōskō - experiential knowing] Him** who has been from the beginning. I am writing to you, young men, because you have overcome the evil one. (emphasis, brackets added)*

Fathers have gone beyond mentally knowing the truth and winning spiritual battles to personally experiencing God. Again, this is an entirely different type of knowledge than just reading about the traits of a good father and applying them.

In the last verse, it does not say that the fathers are old men, but rather, someone who has progressed to deeper intimacy and relational knowledge of God. A relatively young person can be a spiritual mother or father if they have come to know God in a first-hand way.

The Apostle Paul also ties maturity to an experiential knowledge of God. In his letter to the Ephesians, he says leaders are to build up the body of Christ until they *know* God. Knowing God is the path to maturity.

> *Ephesians 4:11-14: And **He gave some [leaders]** as apostles, and some as prophets, and some as evangelists, and some as pastors and teachers, for the equipping of the saints for the work of service, to the building up of the body of Christ; until we all attain to the unity of the faith, and of **the knowledge [epignósis – experiential,***

86

participatory knowledge] of the Son of God, to a mature man, to the measure of the stature which belongs to the fullness of Christ. *As a result, we are no longer to be children,* tossed here and there by waves and carried about by every wind of doctrine, by the trickery of men, by craftiness in deceitful scheming. (emphasis, brackets added)

Spiritual leaders are called to do many things, but their primary task is helping others attain the knowledge of God. So, it goes without saying that developing their own relationship with God is critical; this is how one progresses from a spiritual leader to a spiritual father or mother.

In many Christian circles, the gifts of a leader are highly valued and become a yardstick for measuring their spiritual maturity, rather than Christ's nature within them. A leader may have high-powered gifts and yet have very little emotional maturity. Because of this, they lack a parental nature and are unable to touch someone heart-to-heart.

There is also a community aspect involved in attaining the knowledge of God and maturity. This is why the Apostle Paul instructs leaders to "equip" believers (Eph. 4:12) who then "build up" (Eph. 4:13) their brothers and sisters in Christ, so they come to a greater knowledge of God. There's a sense in which knowledge of God is imparted from one believer to another. We experience Christ by being "unified" (Eph. 4:13) with those who make up the "body of Christ." So, in part, knowledge of God and the maturity it produces comes through connection to other believers.

To a large extent, we cannot reproduce in others what we have not received. If we haven't come to know God, we won't be able to impart His nature to others. We may be able to communicate and disseminate information, but not be able to give this parental nature.

With emotional maturity comes a parental nature and an orientation toward others; a desire to pour into a younger generation. Mature people are secure and settled in their identity so that they can look outside of themselves and parent others. Again, this is an "extra" that the emotionally mature possess.

But this nature is not common among leaders. The Apostle Paul says there are many spiritual "tutors" but few spiritual "fathers."

> *1 **Corinthians** 4:15: For if you were to have **countless tutors** in Christ, yet you would **not have many fathers**, for in Christ Jesus I became your father through the gospel (emphasis added)*

The Scriptures are the plumb line for determining truth from error (2 Tim. 3:16), and the Holy Spirit used Paul to write much of the New Testament. That being said, we can mentally know the Scriptures Paul wrote and still not know God, be mature, or have a parental nature.

Paul had a maturity of heart to go along with his mental knowledge. Listen to Paul's heart of affection for his brothers and sisters in Christ:

> ***Philippians** 1:8: For God is my witness, how I long for you all with the affection of Christ Jesus.*

> ***Philippians** 4:1: Therefore, my brothers and sisters, you whom I love and long for, my joy and crown, stand firm in the Lord in this way, dear friends! (NIV)*

> *1 **Thessalonians** 2:7-8: But we proved to be gentle among you, as a nursing mother tenderly cares for her*

own children. Having so fond an affection for you, we were well-pleased to impart to you not only the gospel of God but also our own lives, because you had become very dear to us.

First the Natural

We experience first in a natural way and then in a spiritual way; this is a Biblical principle at work in our lives.

1 Corinthians 15:46: *However, the spiritual is not first, but the natural; then the spiritual.*

Generally, we receive from our natural parents and other people, and then we receive from God. His plan is that we might experience flesh and blood people, loving and training us, so that we have a basic understanding of His character.

When we have been naturally fathered well, we have an emotional understanding of what a good father is like and more easily make the transition into a spiritual relationship with God. Natural relationships are not to take the place of God, but they do provide a foundation for progressing onto the ultimate relationship with Him.

This principle, *first the natural and then the spiritual*, cuts both directions, positive and negative. Because there's a tendency to view God in the same way as our natural parents, some have a distorted picture of God. If their natural parents were distant or loved them conditionally, they might feel like God is also remote and conditional in His love.

God has placed a great deal of responsibility in the hands of parents and leaders; they are to share His character. Their role is not just to teach people what is true, but to show some of God's nature. In the Scriptures, loving *relationship* and *truth* go together.

Psalm 26:3: *For Your* **lovingkindness** *is before my eyes, and I have walked in Your* **truth**. *(emphasis added)*

Ephesians 4:15: *but speaking* **the truth in love**, *we are to grow up in all aspects into Him who is the head, even Christ. (emphasis added)*

God "Re-Parents" Us

Psalm 68:5: **A father of the fatherless** *and a judge for the widows, is God in His holy habitation. (emphasis added)*

Isaiah 66:13: *"As one whom his* **mother** *comforts, so I will comfort you; And you will be comforted in Jerusalem." (emphasis added)*

Parents and leaders play a crucial role in our development, but if we try to get our ultimate needs met by them, we can miss the Eternal Father and the security He provides. Parents and parental figures are just the springboards into an everlasting relationship with God; there's so much more we get directly from Him.

Jeremiah 31:3: *The LORD appeared to him from afar, saying, "I have loved you with* **an everlasting love**; *Therefore, I have drawn you with lovingkindness." (emphasis added)*

90

For the person who is utterly "forsaken" by their parents, the Lord "receives" them.

Psalm 27:10: *Though my father and mother forsake me, the LORD will receive me. (NIV)*

And for those who've had a mix of good and bad parenting, God fills in emotional deficits and heals wounds from the past; He re-parents them.

But God gives us much more than any human ever could. He has both the perfect nature and perfect knowledge of how to parent us. Our natural parents may have done what "seemed best" when it came to disciplining us, but God knows exactly what we need and how best to give it to us.

Hebrews 12:9-10: *Furthermore, we had earthly fathers to discipline us, and we respected them; shall we not much rather **be subject to the Father of spirits**, and live? For they disciplined us for a short time as **seemed best to them, but He disciplines us for our good**, so that we may share His holiness. (emphasis added)*

God is willing and able to step in and guide us, but we can sometimes be reluctant to allow God to father us. We have become accustomed to protecting ourselves from pain and shame and trying to meet our own emotional needs. So being "subject to the Father of spirits" doesn't enter our minds. It can feel very vulnerable to let God run the show and not be in control. And it can be unnerving when the things we've looked to for emotional security are not working for us.

But our willingness to let God be a father to us is paramount. If we give up our ways of protecting ourselves and any idols we have attached to for emotional security, God will "be a father" to us.

91

*2 Corinthians 6:17-18: Therefore, "Come out from them and be separate, says the Lord. Touch no unclean thing, and I will receive you." And, "I will **be** a Father to you, and you will be my sons and daughters, says the Lord Almighty." (NIV - emphasis added)*

Emotional Trauma from Overt Experiences

God has given us the emotional faculty so we can experience life and relationships. Instead of just knowing truth theoretically, this faculty allows us to feel what is true in a very personal way. For instance, when we feel loved by another person, we are experiencing the fact that we have intrinsic value. Our value as a person is an objective truth that doesn't depend on feelings, but God allows us, through the emotional faculty, to verify and enjoy this truth. We get to experience and feel our value.

With negative experiences and relationships, we might feel things about ourselves that are not true. And when a negative experience is particularly intense, we may feel traumatized emotionally. An experience can be so traumatic that it wounds us emotionally. This emotional wound remains after the experience and poisons our inner man with the message of shame.

Overt trauma comes from negative things that happen to us, as opposed to *covert* trauma, which occurs when we lack positive experiences. Overt trauma might occur when people use words to demean or reject us. Their words, like a sword, can cut into our inner man.

*Proverbs 12:18: There is one who **speaks rashly like the thrusts of a sword,** But the tongue of the wise brings healing. (emphasis added)*

Overt Experience

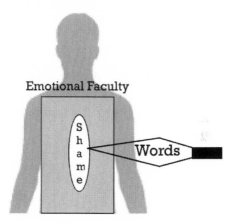

Trauma essentially has to do with being a person. For instance, if you view something destructive happening to a physical building, it's not emotionally traumatic. But the minute the building collapses and hurts a person, it's a different story. The emotional faculty has an acute sensitivity to persons, so we feel it deeply when something bad happens to us or someone else. There's a visceral feeling of violation.

As Christian apologist Ravi Zacharias puts it:

every time the question of evil is raised, it is either by a person or about a person...[16]

93

And because evil is a person-oriented thing, one person has the potential to transmit evil that is damaging to another person. If a car hits us, it may not be emotionally traumatic. But if we find out the person driving that car was careless, we feel it emotionally. It's even more difficult to bear if we find out that a friend was driving the vehicle and intentionally tried to run us down.

Psalms 55:12-13: *For it is not an enemy who reproaches me, then I could bear it; Nor is it one who hates me who has exalted himself against me, then I could hide myself from him. But it is you, a man my equal, my companion and my familiar friend.*

Emotional wounding is a violation of our personhood and comes through relationships. Why is this important? Understanding the nature of wounding helps us to come to a proper view of restoration: *emotional restoration must be personal and relational.* God provides this through union with His Person.

I need to interject an important point. Emotional wounding is not always a result of the bad behavior of others; sometimes, it's our *interpretation* of their behavior that hurts us. And demonic spirits whisper in our ears, telling us the evil intentions people have toward us, in an attempt to devalue and traumatize us.

The most devastating wounding of my childhood came when someone said, over and over again, "You are dumb." The words seemed to cut to my core and haunt me long after the incident. However, my beliefs prior to the experience made me particularly sensitive to these cutting words. I was trying to meet up to unrealistic expectations and standards for myself; I had to have superior intelligence, or in my view, I was worthless. So, it wasn't just someone's demeaning words that hurt me; my standards were

94

already accusing me and made me ripe for an attack. My identity was a house of cards, quickly taken down by a few demonically inspired words. It was partially a self-inflicted wound.

People are responsible for their bad behavior. But ultimately, we are accountable for our internal house. It is best to take responsibility for our feelings, forgive others, and then "fix our eyes on Jesus," who will be the firm foundation for our identity.

Hebrews 12:2: ...fixing our eyes on Jesus, the author and perfecter of faith, who for the joy set before Him endured the cross, despising the shame, and has sat down at the right hand of the throne of God.

Emotional Trauma from Deficits

An impartation is like a pillar that is placed and remains permanently fixed in the emotional faculty.

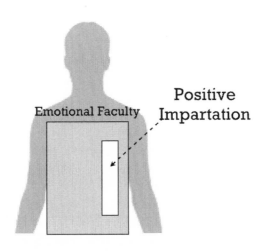

Emotional Faculty

Positive Impartation

Having deficits, or a *lack of good impartations,* in the emotional faculty can cause trauma.

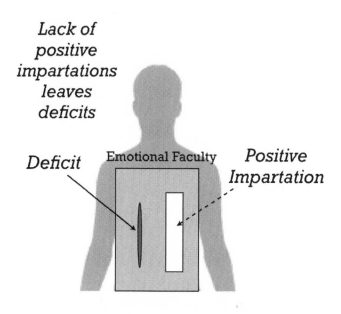

A deficit trauma is hard to identify because it's not linked to any particular experience. In fact, we may not know anything is missing from our soul. But a deficit trauma can be as life-altering as an overt trauma, and the feelings of shame it produces are just as pervasive. Deficits make us question our value, and we feel unworthy of anyone's involvement. There's little confidence that anyone, including God, will step in to support us.

Emotional deficits are specific. If our emotional tank is not filled with fatherly *guidance,* we will lack a measure of internal security in that area. We will have a lingering feeling the ship of life is unsteady, and we are alone at the helm. When the storms of life blow in, it will feel like it's entirely up to us to navigate to a safe harbor.

There's a trauma that goes along with deficits. If we have a guidance deficit, we not only feel like God won't step in to guide us, but we feel like He won't help us because there is something wrong with us. This shameful message takes root in our soul and traumatizes us emotionally.

Some non-Christians have confidence because their soul has received guidance impartations from their natural fathers. They have a general sense that things will work out, it's safe to take risks, and others will help and give direction in their time of need. Impartations deposited into their emotional faculty provide them with a felt sense of security.

Conversely, some children of God are plagued by insecurity because of the lack of impartations from their natural fathers. So, they may feel their Heavenly Father is distant, unconcerned, and displeased with them. They may try to do things to win God's favor and make themselves worthy of His love and leadership. Or they don't expect anything from Him as He seems far away and ambivalent toward them.

Deficits from past relationships, as well as the lack of experiential knowledge of God, can distort the most fundamental truths. Without emotional knowledge of God's nature, we tend to believe lies about Him, how He sees us, and how much He will support and guide us.

Jeremiah 29:11: *For I know the thoughts that I think toward you, says the LORD, thoughts of peace and not of evil, to give you a future and a hope. (NKJV)*

It's not enough to have mental and spiritual knowledge. God wants truth to inhabit the deepest part of our personality; our "innermost being."

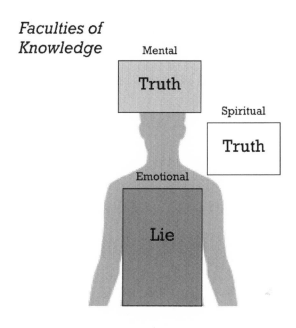

Faculties of Knowledge

Psalm 51:6: *Behold, You desire truth in the innermost being; And in the hidden part You will make me know wisdom.*

The emotional faculty allows us to partake of God; to eat, drink, and taste of His nature. There's something significant and permanent that gets deposited in our souls as we experience God's attributes. The inward man from that point on carries with it a piece of emotional knowledge, like a chip installed into a computer.

This experiential knowledge gives us an internal assurance that changes things. Specific situations and people no longer trigger the same fears and insecurities because we know Christ emotionally. Irrational thoughts about how to make it through life or how to gain God's favor don't consume our minds when we attach to the secure One.

Attaching to God heals our self-image and transforms us into His image. Breathtaking!

2 Corinthians 3:18: *But we all, with unveiled face, beholding as in a mirror the glory of the Lord, are being transformed into the same image from glory to glory, just as from the Lord, the Spirit.*

The "Bottom-Up Approach"

The heart has reasons which reason knows nothing of

~Blaise Pascal

The restoration of the soul starts in the emotional faculty and then moves into our thinking and behaviors.

This "bottom-up approach" runs contrary to the theory that mental and emotional health is controlled by thought alone. Cognitive Behavior Therapy, one of the dominant methods in the field of psychology, requires the identification of irrational thoughts, beliefs, and emotions to modify behavior. It is a kind of top-down approach, using the mind to assess and adjust negative feelings.[17]

Top-down

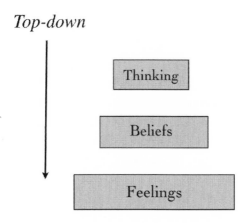

There's a partial truth here. Thoughts that are positive and based on what is rationally true, help to make sense of and bring balance to our emotions.

We see the Cognitive Method in the Bible. The Psalmist mentally reflects on what God has done for Him and then speaks to his emotions, telling them to "return to their rest."

Psalm 116:7: *Return to your rest, O my soul, for the LORD has dealt bountifully with you.*

Although Cognitive Behavioral Therapy has proven to be effective, it has its limits. I believe it is best suited to manage feelings on a short-term basis. It can't restore our emotions or renew our minds. When we've been emotionally wounded and our identity is shaken, it's difficult to think our way into emotional health.

We can't expect the emotional faculty to be renewed and restored through a mental process alone. It would be like blowing your nose and expecting it to take care of a cold; it doesn't address the real problem. Negative thoughts and feelings are often a symptom of damaged emotions or deficits, which cannot be changed by simply adjusting our mental perspective.

Normally the mind is free to operate holistically, balancing the emotions and spirit, but not so with emotional trauma. Trauma creates a crisis in the emotional faculty, which often produces mindsets. Mindsets are thought patterns that tell us what we need to do to prove our value, avoid shame, or feel significant.

Mindsets operate in our thinking but actually *originate* and are *rooted* down in the emotional faculty. They are an outgrowth of negative experiences, feelings, and beliefs.

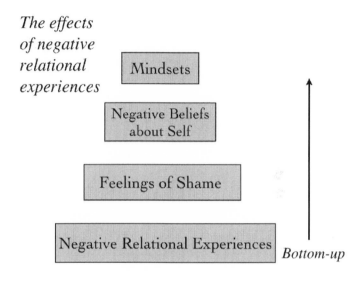

The effects of negative relational experiences

Mindsets

Negative Beliefs about Self

Feelings of Shame

Negative Relational Experiences

Bottom-up

Mindsets are irrational and not based on truth. So, the very thing that we are employing to save the day, *our thinking*, cannot be entirely trusted to make sense of our faulty feelings and beliefs. It's like having a virus in your anti-virus software.

For example, we might have feelings of worthlessness, so a mindset develops in our thinking, which requires us to perform to be valuable. Our mind is giving us a false view of reality, yet we are counting on it to make sense of things. Can you see the dilemma? A mindset gives us incorrect directives and information and doesn't allow for any deviation from a specific solution. So, it's challenging to maintain clear, objective thoughts required for the Cognitive Method.

Even if we correctly identify false feelings and beliefs, it doesn't heal or transform our inner person. We essentially have an emotional and relational problem. Emotional wounding comes through relational experiences, and emotional healing must also come by relational experiences.

The heart comes to know truth and is transformed through a person-to-person relationship with the Father, Son, and Holy Spirit. The mind then follows suit and is renewed. So, our thinking, and ultimately, our behaviors, are driven from the bottom up.

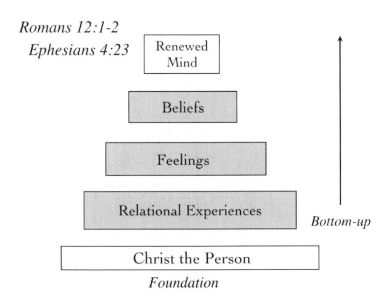

God has predetermined that emotional, spiritual, and mental health would flow out of a bridal-type relationship with Himself. Making Christ the foundation of our souls by developing a heart attachment to Him will restore and transform us into His image.

CHAPTER FOUR

SHAME

Shame is the message that we lack intrinsic value. It tells us that we are worthless, broken beyond repair, unredeemable, and unlovable. The feeling of shame is so intense that it cuts to the core of our being.

The emotional faculty is where we experience the truth that we are loved, valuable, and significant. Our intrinsic value can be felt. But because we live in a fallen world, not all our relational experiences are positive. There are times when instead of feeling that we are valuable, we feel that we are shameful.

Much of what we do in life is an effort to push back against this terrible feeling. Shame creates an identity crisis that consumes our thoughts and influences our motivations and behaviors.

People will spend their time, energy, resources, and talents trying to defend themselves from the toxic shame message. Shame is such an unbearable feeling that humans will do just about anything to avoid it.

*Proverbs 18:14: The human spirit can endure in sickness, but **a crushed spirit who can bear?** (NIV - emphasis added)*

Unfortunately, when emotions are damaged, feelings of shame are not a one-time occurrence. Shame imbeds in wounded emotions, and its dark message persists until the emotions are restored.

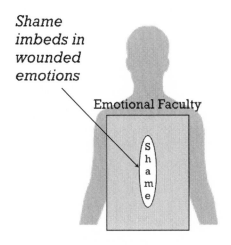

Shame imbeds in wounded emotions

Emotional Faculty

Shame

Most people are unaware of how much shame is affecting their lives. A businessman came to me one time deeply upset because his company wasn't growing. He said, "Bruce, I don't think shame is the issue; I'm concerned because my business isn't doing well."

But behind his intense emotional reaction to the decline in his business, shame was rearing its head. Long ago, this businessman determined that success in business would be a way to affirm his value and protect himself from shame.

This businessman's mindset was doomed to fail from the beginning. As soon as there was a little downturn in his business, the feelings of shame resurfaced. Panic set in because his personal value seemed to hang in the balance with the success or failure of the company.

We saw the power of shame when we met a woman called to be a missionary in a dangerous part of the world. She was full of anxiety as she pondered a trip to this foreign land. At first, we thought this was simply a survival instinct as it was natural for her to have some fear regarding her physical wellbeing in this particular country.

However, after probing deeper, we found she was afraid of being shamed. Although concerned about a physical assault, it was what an attack would mean that really disturbed her. An attack on the mission field would confirm her worst fears: she was not worthy of God's protection and would be abandoned. She actually had more fear of re-experiencing the shame than she did of losing her life.

Trauma from the past was influencing her perspective. When she was a child, her parents died. She felt God took them because He didn't care for her, and she also felt that her parents abandoned her because she was not valuable. These messages of shame had embedded in her emotions. Although she realized these feelings were irrational and not in line with her Biblical theology, the fear of shame still gripped her heart.

In a similar situation, we knew two young women who went on a short-term mission trip in a part of the world hostile to Christians.When we received the news that things had "gone bad" and the women were very "troubled," we assumed they had been assaulted physically in some way. But later we found out they were shaken because the trip was "uneventful." Why all the intense emotions surrounding a lackluster trip? Shame. These young ladies viewed their unmet expectations on the mission field as a personal failure. They were evaluating themselves and their value as a person on how effective they were as missionaries.

Again, the fear of shame was more intense for these women than the fear of violence. These brave women were willing to give their lives for the sake of the Gospel in a dangerous country, but when back in safe territory, they were stalked by feelings of shame.

Protecting the Shame

Emotional wounding causes us to feel shame. Mindsets are unconscious defense mechanisms that develop in our thinking to fight off these feelings of shame.

When there is trauma and wounding, the mind goes into a protective mode and offers solutions to this emotional crisis.

Mind offers solutions for pain and shame in the emotions

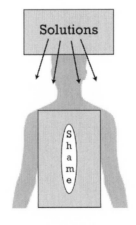

The person might have thoughts like, "Success will make you feel significant" or "Avoiding people will protect you from rejection and shame."

If a person *depends* on that solution for emotional security, the mind becomes "conformed" (Rom. 12:2) to that false view. The mind's protective solution becomes a *mindset.*

Solution becomes a mindset

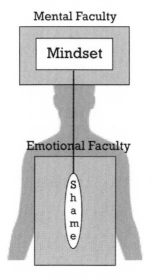

Mental Faculty

Mindset

Emotional Faculty

Shame

Once a person trusts in a solution and a mindset has formed, that particular solution becomes the one and only answer for shame. The mindset creates tunnel vision, keeping the person focused on one solution and ignoring everything else.

Like a reflex, the mindset reacts automatically and instantly when it hones in on perceived "threats." Operating at an unconscious level, it searches the environment for someone or something that might cause the person to re-experience shame. Before a person has time to surmise the situation consciously, the mindset will tell them what they must do or not do to avoid shame. They are convinced they have to comply with the dictates of their mindset, or else they will be vulnerable to re-experiencing shame.

There are many different kinds of mindsets we can depend on to protect ourselves from feeling shame. A person may have a performance mindset, which requires them to constantly meet high standards, while another might have a withdrawal mindset, which tells them to avoid people and activities.

If the protective mindset has to do with control, the person will feel that losing control makes them vulnerable to shame. If one were to suggest they transfer control into God's hands, their first instinct would be to resist this option because it makes them feel too vulnerable.

As long as the wounding and shame remain in the emotions, the mindset remains intact. This brings us to a critical point: the only way a mindset can be removed is through the restoration of the emotions.

So, what do we do with feelings of shame? Some Christians believe owning their feelings of shame is the answer. They believe all their identity problems will be solved if they resign themselves to being a worthless creature. They cite Apostle Paul's comment, "Nothing good dwells in me" as evidence that they don't possess intrinsic value. But Paul is clearly saying that there is no good thing dwelling in his "flesh." Clearly, the Spirit of God dwelled in Paul, so he wasn't saying there was not anything good in him whatsoever.

*Romans 7:18: For I know that nothing good dwells in me, that is, **in my flesh**; for the willing is present in me, but the doing of the good is not. (emphasis added)*

Self-degradation can just be a backdoor approach to fighting off feelings of shame. Paradoxically, some folks are searching for value by downplaying their value. No matter how you slice it, this is still an attempt to fight off feelings of shame. Paul says this kind of false humility is a way to "puff" oneself up. It is a form of pride.

Colossians 2:18: Do not let anyone who delights in false humility and the worship of angels disqualify you. Such a person also goes into great detail about what they have seen; they are puffed up with idle notions by their unspiritual mind. (NIV)

Confronting shame head-on with God is the best approach. If we allow Him to restore us emotionally and cleanse us of shame, we will no longer feel the need to prove our value or protect ourselves.

As long as we are focused on doing something to feel valuable, the message of shame stays firmly fixed in our souls. When we try to cover the shame and earn acceptance, the inner man remains unhealed and feelings of unworthiness persist. If we stay attached to our mindsets, we are unable to experience God's unconditional love for us. But this is precisely what many of us do when we are wounded emotionally.

This tendency to self-protect goes back to Adam and Eve when they defended themselves by blaming and hiding (Gen. 3:8-13). Their self-protection was a sin beyond eating the forbidden fruit. The cover-up was truly as bad as the crime. Instead of trusting God to restore their sense of righteousness and value, they clothed themselves with leaves (Gen. 3:7). This sin of independence and lack of trust in God's goodness was the reason for their initial rebellion and their self-protection.

God was gracious in providing restoration for Adam and Eve. He clothed them with animal skins (Gen. 3:21), symbolizing the sacrifice of Jesus at the cross and being clothed in His righteousness.

Just like Adam and Eve, we often clothe ourselves with different things to cover up our shame. We sew leaves for ourselves by trying to measure up to standards, seeking someone's approval, or avoiding things. Not only did Adam and Eve disobey God and try to cover their shame, but they also pulled away from Him. This is a sinister aspect of shame; it makes us want to hide from God, which cuts us off from the Person who can heal our hearts. It seems the last thing we want to do is face God when we feel shame. We'd rather do things to prove our value or hide altogether. Sometimes we feel more comfortable doing things for God than opening ourselves up to Him.

Getting to the Lord can be a challenge when our shame is saying, "Stay away!" Sometimes we need to go back to the elementary principles and draw clear lines between who we are and what we do. Using our mental faculty to focus on the objective, Biblical truth that God unconditionally loves us can help us go to Him with our feelings of shame.

Once we are vulnerable with the Lord and actually meet Him, things change. We realize we have intrinsic value. And it becomes clear that being near to God is beneficial; it is "our good."

*Psalm 73:28: But as for me, **the nearness of God is my good**; I have made the Lord GOD my refuge, that I may tell of all Your works. (emphasis added)*

Even if we have done something wrong and need correction, God doesn't condemn or shame us. The Holy Spirit is a master at convicting us of sin while at the same time allowing us to hold onto our value as a person.

When it comes to shame, there are only two options: God's way or our way. We can "put on the Lord" and allow Him to restore us, or we can stick to the protective mindsets of our "flesh" and lose the battle with shame.

Romans 13:14: *But put on the Lord Jesus Christ and make no provision for the flesh in regard to its lusts.*

Shame's Relationship to Strengths

We often experience shame related to our strengths. A strength is an area where we have spiritual and mental abilities, as well as an emotional value for that strength. This emotional value gives us a passion and desire to use our strength, but it also makes us vulnerable to shame. How does this play out? When a leader, who naturally values leadership, isn't led well by others, they tend to feel shame. They might feel: *My dad, coach, teacher, or pastor isn't leading me well, so I must not be worthy of leadership.* Because leadership is so important to them, if they are not led well, they assume it's because the other person doesn't value them.

Another shame trap many fall into is measuring their value based on how *effectively* they use their strength. The leader views leadership as being of utmost importance, so if they underperform as a leader, they feel shame. In their view, it may be ok to stumble in some areas of life, but certainly not as a leader!

But God never intended us to use our strength to feel better about ourselves or as a way to gauge our value as a person. Using the strength in this way creates an endless cycle where feelings of shame are never resolved. Even if we use our strength perfectly, it won't provide the security that God has for us.

A Demonic Weapon

The devil tried to use shame as a weapon against Jesus in Matthew 4:3, when he said to Him, "If You are the Son of God, command that these stones become bread." In other words: *prove that you are the eternal Son of God, who is infinitely valuable.*

But Jesus wouldn't be caught in a shame-trap. He refused to perform a miracle to prove that He was the Son of God, but rather looked to the Father for His identity and security. Jesus' response to the devil in Matthew 4:4 was, "It is written, 'Man shall not live on bread alone, but on every word that proceeds out of the mouth of God.'" Jesus knew that through His connection to the Father, He would experience life, security, and acceptance, so He didn't try to establish his identity independent of the Father.

When Jesus walked on earth, He gave us an example of how to live with a heart attachment to Father God. He also showed us how to submit to the Father's will as He endured the cross. But He rejected the shame that was associated with His sufferings; He despised the shame.

> **Hebrews 12:2:** *...fixing our eyes on Jesus, the author and perfecter of faith, who for the joy set before Him endured the cross, **despising the shame**, and has sat down at the right hand of the throne of God. (emphasis added)*

Demonic spirits try to use shame against us because they understand the power of shame. They know that if they can wound us and plant the seeds of shame in our souls, we will do just about anything to avoid this feeling. We will be tempted to attach to a mindset to defend ourselves and try to prove we have value.

Shame is a powerful internal message that demands a response. Like it or not, we will do something to avoid this feeling. If we try to fight this enemy by ourselves, the war will inevitably be lost. But if we attach our hearts to God and allow Him to restore our emotions, this dark internal foe will be conquered.

Case Study: "The Woman of Balance"

Joanne is a woman who brings harmony to people and situations and has an intuitive sense when things are out of balance. Her friends love her even approach to life and often ask her for advice. On top of that, Joanne has a warm, loving quality about her.

As is the case with most people, Joanne's strength is also her greatest vulnerability. Her father and mother are extremely volatile and unpredictable. Because she has a natural inclination for harmony, the lack of stability in her daily life is especially difficult. Her mother is irrational and always making nonsensical, contradictory statements. Her father is quiet for long periods, but then suddenly erupts with a torrent of emotion.

The household is also spiritually confusing. Sometimes her parents are insistent on church attendance, and other times they are dabbling in the occult and making decisions based on horoscopes.

Although most of the household conflict is not directly related to Joanne, she is still affected by it. Initially, the chaotic environment rattles her nerves, but eventually, it affects her at a more personal level as she begins to question the reason for the chaos. Her feelings and demonic spirits tell her, "If you were loved, your parents would provide a balanced environment." Joanne buys into a lie that the lack of harmony surrounding her life is her fault; she believes she is shameful.

To protect herself from this shame, Joanne chooses to become the ultimate peacemaker. Because her gift is bringing harmony, this comes easily for her. A mindset develops in her thinking, which has her appeasing everyone and constantly trying to avoid any conflict.

This mindset hurts her relationships. When there is tension, real or perceived, her mindset presses her to make peace, so she often holds back her true feelings. When someone is the least bit disagreeable, Joanne reflexively tries to calm them down and takes on a false sense of responsibility. Her friends feel they don't know her true self because she rarely reveals what's going on inside herself.

When Joanne becomes exhausted by taking care of everyone and always being the peacemaker, she decides to seek counsel. A Christian counselor questions her as to why she is giving so much. Joanne responds with, "I thought I was supposed to bring peace and harmony to everyone. And my parents always told me that true spirituality was all about loving people."

Joanne's life is further confused because she incorporates several religions into her life. She picks and chooses from a variety of spiritual approaches and then keeps her focus on what she believes matters the most: good works.

Bringing balance, harmony, and love to people are all good traits and part of Joanne's calling. But there's a toxic mix because she uses her harmony gift for self-protection. Joanne's counselor suggests she seek out a personal relationship with Jesus and search the Scriptures for truth.

Joanne's life changes dramatically after she commits her life to Jesus. In her study of the Bible, she sees there is "discernment" in how to administer her love, and she begins to seek the Holy Spirit's guidance for how to best love others:

Philippians 1:9: And this I pray, that your love may abound still more and more in real knowledge and all discernment.

117

Reading the Scriptures brings comfort to Joanne; she loves to learn about God and meditate on His wonderful attributes. Whenever she has a question about anything, she opens her Bible and searches for answers. Over time Joanne's shelves are filled with a collection of Bibles, commentaries, and devotionals. One of her favorite verses is:

Psalm 119:105: Your word is a lamp to my feet and a light to my path.

Joanne loves the fact that God's Word lights her path and brings balance and boundaries to her life. But there is also something going on inside. As she experiences the God who is full of balance and harmony, her inner person is restored. With this internal change, she no longer feels the pressure to use balance as a way to protect herself from shame or prove her value as a person. The mindset that pressed her to bring harmony doesn't plague her thoughts anymore.

CHAPTER FIVE

MINDSETS

Double-Minded

Mindsets are a powerful force within the human soul. A mindset is a defense mechanism in our thinking, a thought pattern that develops to protect our emotions.

After a mindset forms, there are essentially two ways of thinking in the mind. A dysfunctional way of thinking (a mindset) and a healthy way of thinking coexist.

The healthy part of the mind can think freely, unencumbered by emotional issues. It's capable of thinking broadly and objectively because it's not pre-occupied with self-protection. The healthy mind also receives new information with relative ease. For instance, say a person thinks that reincarnation is true. But later they become a Christian and learn from the Word of God that they only "die once."

Hebrews 9:27: *And inasmuch as it is appointed for men to die once and after this comes judgment*

After reading this Scripture passage, inaccurate information is exchanged for accurate information. Because this part of the mind freely accepts new knowledge and truth, one bit of data is replaced with another. So "renewing" (Rom. 12:1) the healthy part of the mind is a fairly straightforward process.

When it comes to a mindset, things are not so simple. Mindsets have developed because of an emotional crisis and are anchored in the emotional faculty. A mindset's sole reason for existence is to fight off feelings of shame. However, it's ultimately unable to do this.

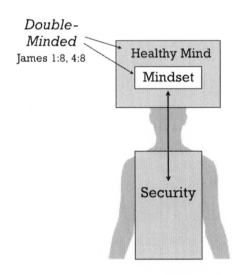

After a mindset develops, there's what the Bible calls a "double-mindedness" (James 1:8, 4:8) operating in our souls. Sometimes we think clearly, and other times our mindset is in operation.

These two parts of the mind can be in direct opposition to one another. For example, a leader thinks in terms of leadership in their healthy mind, but can also have a mindset telling them, "do not lead."

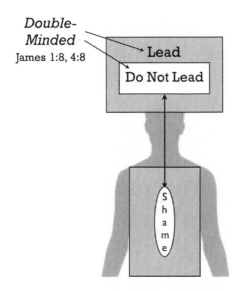

The leader has a God-given ability to understand leadership concepts; they naturally know how to influence, inspire, and direct people. But when they are wounded emotionally, they might try to protect themselves by *not leading*. It may feel too vulnerable to influence people or cast a vision for an organization. A mindset (*do not lead*) presses them to avoid leadership as a protective measure.

So, there's a double-mindedness, where healthy thinking and protective thinking contradict one another. The leader may be thinking about leading, and suddenly, their mindset shuts down these thoughts and tries to get them to avoid leadership roles. Other times the two parts of the mind operate simultaneously, struggling against each other in a sort of mental wrestling match.

What's the answer to this mental quagmire? The Apostle James admonishes the double-minded to "purify their *hearts*."

> **James 4:8:** *Draw near to God and He will draw near to you. Cleanse your hands, you sinners; and **purify your hearts, you double-minded**. (emphasis added)*

Purify literally means to make one's heart "chaste."[18] The idea here is of a wife having a pure devotion to her husband. In other words, we are to trust God, our true Husband, to meet our heart needs and help us to overcome shame.

Mindsets develop because of a misdirected heart. If we trust in something other than God, even if it's behavior on our part, to protect ourselves or to feel valuable, we will remain double-minded. God alone reserves the right to be our savior; He is the jealous Bridegroom who wants to give us heart security.

Heart Leads the Head

All of our reasoning ends in surrender to feeling

~Blaise Pascal

The heart leading the head is a pattern seen throughout Scripture. Whatever we believe, embrace, attach to, or put our trust in from the heart, ultimately shapes our thinking. Transformation, restoration, and renewal require a bottom-up approach.

The mind does affect emotions, and it is healthy for the mind to lead the emotions at times. But in the long haul, what we love and worship directly affects our thinking. The heart *leads* the head.

If we embrace God, we can comprehend truth more clearly. But if our hearts are attached to other things, whether it be people or ideologies, our minds will be fixed on those things. And, ultimately, we will be unable to grasp truth mentally.

Why is this principle so important? The wholeness and balance of our souls hinge on where we *set our hearts*. We cannot think clearly, or possess a right view of life, without a proper heart attachment to God.

So now let's look at what the Holy Spirit says, through the Scriptures, about the heart leading the head.

In Romans, there is a reference to those who do not "honor" God from their heart. This results in them becoming "futile in their speculations" (their thinking):

Romans 1:21: *For even though they knew God, they did* **not honor Him as God** *or give thanks, but they became* **futile in their speculations***, and their foolish heart was darkened. (emphasis added)*

Paul makes it clear that Christians are just as vulnerable as unbelievers ("Gentiles") to the heart leading the head.

> **Ephesians 4:17-18:** *So this I say, and affirm together with the Lord, that you walk no longer just as the Gentiles also walk, in the **futility of their mind, being darkened in their understanding**, excluded from the life of God because of the ignorance that is in them, **because of the hardness of their heart.** (emphasis added)*

In the following verse, we see God "giving people over to a depraved mind" when they do not "acknowledge" Him as God:

> **Romans 1:28:** *And just as they did not see fit to **acknowledge God** any longer, God gave them over to a **depraved mind**, to do those things which are not proper, (emphasis added)*

In Isaiah, there is a similar *giving over*. God allows a man to be confused in his thinking after he has made an attachment to an idol. The process starts *in the heart:* he "worships," "bows down," and "prays" to the idol. And he trusts it to "save" him; to provide heart security.

> **Isaiah 44:17:** *And the rest of it he makes into a god. To blocks of wood he **bows down, worships, prays,** and says, "**Save me**, since you are my god." (ISV - emphasis added)*

After he has made a heart attachment to the idol, he loses understanding of reality. He can't *think* straight, and it seems rational to trust "blocks of wood." There's an inability to mentally comprehend the most basic truth; there's a "lie in his right hand," yet he can't see it.

*Isaiah 44:18-20: They don't realize; they don't understand, because their **eyes are plastered over so they cannot see, and their minds, too, so they cannot understand. No one stops to think. No one has the knowledge or understanding to think—yes to think!—** "Half of it I burned in the fire. I even baked bread on its coals, and I roasted meat and ate it. And am I about to make detestable things from what is left? **Am I about to bow down to blocks of wood?"** He tends ashes. **A deceived mind has lead him astray. It cannot be his life, nor can he say, "There's a lie in my right hand."** (ISV - emphasis added)*

In the following verse, an "unbelieving heart" leads to a "defiled mind":

*Titus 1:15: To the pure, all things are pure; but to those who are defiled and **unbelieving**, nothing is pure, but both their **mind** and their conscience are defiled. (emphasis added)*

When Jesus performed the miracle of the loaves of bread, the disciples lacked understanding. They couldn't comprehend something that happened right in front of their eyes.

*Mark 6:52: for they had **not understood** about the loaves; their **hearts were hardened**. (NIV - emphasis added)*

Their lack of mental understanding of the miracle is attributed to hardened hearts. The Greek word for "understood" in this verse has to do with *mental* comprehension.[19] The mind is unable to understand because of the attitude or condition of the heart.

What does the Bible say about positively changing our thinking so we have clear mental comprehension? The heart-leading-the-head principle is at work in what the Apostle Paul refers to as the "renewal of the mind."

> **Romans 12:1-2: I beseech you** therefore, brethren, by the mercies of God, that ye **present your bodies a living sacrifice**, holy, acceptable unto God, which is your reasonable service. And be not conformed to this world: but be ye transformed by the **renewing of your mind**, that ye may prove what is that good, and acceptable, and perfect, will of God. (KJV - emphasis added)

The renewal of the mind follows a change of heart.

First, Paul says, I "beseech you," which is an appeal to the believer's *will*. Paul is pleading with the believer to yield to God. Unless a person gives God control and chooses to submit to Him, a renewal process won't happen.

Second, Paul says, "present yourselves as a living sacrifice," referring to the believers giving themselves entirely to God: body, soul, and spirit. This is an act of worship as the Bride says to the Bridegroom, "Lord, I give myself wholly to you."

The renewing of the mind requires and is preceded by a *willing* and *worshipful* heart.

A "Conformed" Mind

The Apostle Paul says that we should not be "conformed to this world," but "be transformed by the renewing of the mind" (Rom. 12:2, KJV).

If we have a heart-dependence on the "world's way" of doing things, it will eventually work its way up into our thinking. When we believe we are valuable because we have possessions, power, or prestige, our mind becomes locked into, *conformed to*, that belief. The principle of the heart leading the head will be at work in our souls in a negative way. Once we have embraced from the heart a false belief, our mind becomes conformed to that belief. We become convinced, in our thinking, that belief is real and true.

If we believe in our hearts that controlling people is the only way to feel secure, we will eventually come to *think* that it is true. It becomes our default position, and we will find it difficult to mentally grasp any other solution than control. Even though it doesn't work or line up with reality, a conformed mind will take us back to the same solution over and over again. It has us trapped in a catch-22.

Or if we believe achievement will bring ultimate satisfaction, eventually, we become trapped into thinking that it's the only path to fulfillment. Our conformed mind will have us in pursuit of achievements, even though it never satisfies.

I recall a man who was extremely performance-driven. Everything, both in his work and personal life, was done to be "successful." Of course, he was never able to achieve enough and was, in fact, very insecure. When I suggested he depended on success to satisfy an emotional need, he struggled to understand what I was getting at. Although he was very intelligent, his mind seemed to be in a fog when it came to this topic. And it was a fairly simple concept: *you are trying to get security through performance*. But he couldn't see it; it was as if he was trying to understand the theory of relativity.

Once the mind has been conformed to a mindset, it's tough to think outside of its paradigm. The mind is boxed into a distorted view, and unless a person is willing to redirect their *heart*, the mental fog remains.

Whatever we have our heart set on eventually influences every aspect of our character. The thing we love and put our trust in permeates our entire being. Ultimately, we will become like the idol we have embraced.

> *2 **Kings** 17:15: They rejected his decrees and the covenant he had made with their ancestors and the statutes he had warned them to keep. **They followed worthless idols and themselves became worthless.** They imitated the nations around them although the LORD had ordered them, "Do not do as they do." (NIV – emphasis added)*

> *Jeremiah 2:5: This is what the LORD says: "What fault did your ancestors find in me, that they strayed so far from me? They **followed worthless idols** and **became worthless themselves**." (NIV – emphasis added)*

> *Psalm 115:8: **Those who make them [idols] will become like them**, everyone who trusts in them. (emphasis, brackets added)*

The heart-leading-the-head principle also works positively. If we make a heart attachment to God, we will be transformed into His image and will think like Him. Choosing to love God and attach to Him changes us at the core. It affects every area of our life: thinking, motivations, behaviors, and destiny.

Jean and I have seen people suddenly realize, almost like an outside observer, that they have a mindset operating. A light bulb goes on, and they see their mind is presenting a particular worldview and a specific solution for their emotional needs. Frequently, they ask, "How do I stop my mind from thinking this way?" Our answer: "You can't renew your mind just by trying to change your thinking. You need a process of the heart and a new attachment of the heart."

Influencers of Mindsets

A mindset is the mental faculty's way of trying to help out the emotional faculty, albeit in a dysfunctional way. But mindsets don't form randomly; there are outside forces that influence the type of mindset a person chooses.

Here are some influences: a person's strength, family, culture, generational spirits, and territorial spirits.

Influencers of Mindsets

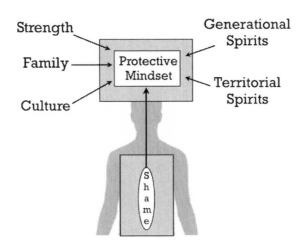

Strength Influences Mindsets

Typically, the first thing a person reaches for when emotionally wounded is their God-given strength. What does the planner do when they experience shame? They plan!

A planner believes that if they shine as a planner, it will offset feelings of shame and provide a sense of value. Using the strength in this way is tempting because it comes so easily and is naturally part of their value system. Once they believe their value as a person is directly related to their effectiveness as a planner, a mindset forms. They then become trapped, as it were, in their thinking. The mindset tells them they can't afford to fail as a planner. Eventually, the weight of such a burden takes its toll.

This tendency to lean too much on the strength is common to all personality types. Most people have a mindset that requires using their strength to protect themselves, create value, or meet their emotional needs.

Family Influences Mindsets

Much of what we view as important in life comes from our families. So, we tend to place our trust in their values, and when these values are not God-centered, they become fuel for mindsets.

A family might believe the amount of money you make or the type of job you have gives you significance.

Another family may believe that family connections provide an ultimate sense of security. "Blood is thicker than water," so family relationships must be held together at any cost.

And then another family believes hard work is the measure of a person's value, so one must always be laboring.

These family messages are often part of the formation of a mindset. A person may attach to a family value when shame rears its ugly head or when they are looking for a way to meet their heart's needs. For instance, if someone starts questioning their significance, they may attach to their family's belief that they must have prestige in the community to be significant. A mindset will then have them buying a fancy house and trying to get into an exclusive country club to feel significant.

Because a person's family of origin is such a powerful influencer, it can be difficult to turn away from their ungodly beliefs and to trust in God.

Culture Influences Mindsets

People are inundated by the messages of their surrounding culture. It presents a worldview: what it means to be valuable as a person, as well as what's required to be safe, significant, sanctified, and satisfied.

For instance, American culture is steeped in materialism, so the citizen is told, in various ways, that acquiring material possessions will provide them with a sense of value and security. American culture also values individualism, so the culture declares that if you are a unique and special individual, you will have ultimate significance.

Asian cultures, on the other hand, esteem conformity to the group. These cultures say unity and allegiance to the group will keep one safe, and you need to be accepted by the group to have ultimate value.

Cultural messages often influence where a person places their trust, and thus the kind of mindset that develops in their thinking.

Now, just because a person has an intellectual agreement with a cultural value does not mean they have a mindset in operation. For example, someone may think that materialism is an essential thing in life, but they later realize it isn't very meaningful. Because they haven't put their *trust* in materialism from the heart, their false thoughts about the importance of materialism are easily changed. But a mindset is something altogether different. If someone trusts in materialism as a way to feel valuable, a mindset develops. Or if someone depends on something like individualism to feel significant, a mindset forms.

These mindsets are rooted in the emotions and don't give way easily. Once the affections of the heart are aligned with an ungodly, cultural ideology, the mind follows suit. We are trapped in a thought pattern and deceived into thinking that something will help us when it cannot.

Cultural values can't protect us or meet our emotional needs. When we trust in a societal value rather than God, we end up being "tossed" about and "unstable in all our ways."

> **James 1:6-8:** *But he must ask in faith without any doubting, for **the one who doubts** is like the surf of the sea, driven and **tossed by the wind**. For that man ought not to expect that he will receive anything from the Lord, being a double-minded man, **unstable** in all his ways. (emphasis added)*

Stepping back from one's culture is not easy when everyone seems to be flowing down the same ideological river. But the benefits of turning our backs on cultural idols are great. If we set our affections on the Most High God and trust Him, we will be emotionally secure, and our thinking will come into alignment with truth.

Demonic Spirits Influence Mindsets

Demonic forces work full-time influencing our thoughts. Their goal is to lure us into ungodly *emotional* attachments, which turn into mindsets.

Demonic spirits often start by questioning God's character and trustworthiness. If they can get us to trust in an idol, we won't see God clearly, and the experience and comprehension of Him will be lost. In this way, we "turn away from God's love."

> **Jonah 2:8:** *"Those who cling to worthless idols turn away from God's love for them." (NIV)*

One dire consequence of trusting in something other than God is that we lose *perception* of Him. As C.S. Lewis says, we see God "through our whole self." So, when we have a mindset operating within our souls, we don't see God clearly; we are viewing Him through a "dirty telescope."

> *...[God] shows much more of Himself to some people than to others - not because He has favorites, but because it is impossible for Him to show Himself to a man whose whole mind and character are in the wrong condition. Just as sunlight, though it has no favorites, cannot be reflected in a dusty mirror as clearly as a clean one.*
>
> *You can put this another way by saying that while in other sciences the instruments you use are things external to yourself (things like microscopes and telescopes), the instruments through which you see God is your whole self. And if a man's self is not kept clean and bright, his glimpse of God will be blurred - like the Moon seen through a dirty telescope. That is why horrible nations have horrible religions: they have been looking at God through a dirty lens.[20]*

Once a mindset has developed, evil spirits have us right where they want us. They simply fan the flames of the ungodly fire (the mindset) we have started in our souls. When we have a success mindset, demons torment us with evaluations about the success of our business or marriage or career. Our belief system is used against us, as demons have us reviewing every aspect of our lives and pointing out every failure.

Demonic forces use all means available to propagate their lies. One of their entry points into the human soul is an open door that exists because of sins and idolatry of ancestors.

> **Exodus 20:5:** "You shall not worship them or serve them; for I, the LORD your God, am a jealous God, visiting the iniquity of the fathers on the children, on the third and the fourth generations of those who hate Me."

For instance, if a person uses *control* to avoid rejection, their children, grandchildren, and great-grandchildren will also become vulnerable to the same sin pattern. A spiritual door is opened to a familiar spirit, *a spirit of control*, which influences from one generation to another.

Notice, in the following verse, that the parents' sin of "harlotry" has a spirit attached to it, which tempts the *daughters* to "play the harlot."

> **Hosea 4:10-13:** *They will eat, but not have enough; **They will <u>play the harlot</u>**, but not increase, because they have stopped giving heed to the LORD. Harlotry, wine and new wine take away the understanding. My people consult their wooden idol, and their diviner's wand informs them; **For a <u>spirit of harlotry</u> has led them astray**, and they have played the harlot, from their God. They offer sacrifices on the tops of the mountains and burn incense on the hills, under oak, poplar and terebinth, because their shade is pleasant. **<u>Therefore your</u>***

daughters* play *the harlot *and your brides commit adultery. (emphasis added)*

Because of a familiar spirit's influence, the same idolatry, sins, and mindsets often continue from one generation to another.

Demonic spirits also influence through geographical strongholds. In this Biblical text from the book of Daniel, an angel is speaking about warfare with "princes," or territorial spirits, that are influencing kingdoms.

Daniel 10:20: *Then he said, "Do you understand why I came to you? But I shall now return to fight against the* **prince of Persia***; so I am going forth, and behold, the* **prince of Greece** *is about to come. (emphasis added)*

Indeed, there are hierarchies of demonic forces influencing both large and small regions.

Ephesians 6:12: *For our struggle is not against flesh and blood, but against the* **rulers***, against the* **powers***, against the world* **forces** *of this darkness, against the spiritual forces of wickedness in the heavenly places. (emphasis added)*

These territorial spirits bombard the thoughts and emotions of people who live or travel into locales. Their influence may be as small as a city block or as large as a country.

Demons present a worldview in a geographical area, including ungodly views about what is *important*, what *success* looks like, how to ensure *safety*, how to achieve *significance*, and how to be *sanctified*.

Promoting and then entrapping people into sinful behavior is just part of their agenda. Demons' *primary* goal is to distort the knowledge of God. A proper understanding of God is key to everything, so these hosts of hell come at people with "sophisticated arguments" against the "true knowledge of God."

2 Corinthians 10:5: *We are destroying sophisticated arguments and every exalted and proud thing that sets itself up against the [true] knowledge of God, and we are taking every thought and purpose captive to the obedience of Christ (Amplified Bible)*

After establishing a stronghold in a geographical area, these spirits present a distorted and ungodly view of reality. In one area, it might be: "Being famous will give you significance." In another region: "Physical beauty gives you value." Or another territory: "Having a union job keeps you safe."

When people spend the majority of their lives in a location and hear the same lie year after year, they often develop mindsets related to the demonic stronghold in that region.

Let's say there's a demonic stronghold in a town related to *education.* "Educational attainment equals personal value," is the spirit's constant message to the residents of the township. After being exposed to this spirit, someone may trust in education for heart security, which then turns into a mindset: *I am valuable if I am highly educated.*

The battle in the spiritual world is for heart allegiance. Demons, whether they be generational or territorial, are essentially urging people to trust in something other than God for their heart security. These dark forces understand that once people take the bait and trust in an idol, a mindset will develop. The person then has their worst enemy inside themselves; their mindset torments and obscures their view of God.

Beware of no man more than of yourself;

we carry our worst enemies within us

~Charles Spurgeon

Loss of Mental Capacity

A mindset, much like a virus in a computer, interferes with the mind's ability to function at full capacity. Because part of the mind is busy with thoughts about protection, the rest of the mind is unable to work as clearly and broadly as designed.

Some folks are by nature highly creative but don't use the creative part of their minds (right-brain function) much. They have a mindset focusing on practical things (left-brain function). Say a person has a mindset such as, *keep things in order to feel secure.* They will find it challenging to use their creative thinking because their mindset, *keeping things in order*, is all about practical thinking.

Another person's mindset might be: *I will only feel significant if I'm creative.* It focuses on the creative side while staying clear of practical thinking. So, this person may have all sorts of creative ideas, but they can't seem to get their big-picture thoughts into a practical format.

In other instances, thinking is disabled. If someone is ridiculed as a child when they are involved in some creative endeavor, they may resolve *never to create again.* After making this inner vow, a part of their thinking is effectively shut down, and so they struggle to think creatively.

I recall an aspiring orchestra composer who found the practical part of his thinking was shut down. He created beautiful music in his mind, but to his frustration, couldn't get his ideas on paper. When he was a child, his father belittled his ideas, so he vowed he would *avoid criticism by keeping his ideas to himself.* Years later, as a middle-aged person, he desired to write down his wonderful musical compositions, but his mindset wouldn't allow it. In his words, he had a "mental block" every time he tried to express his ideas.

These kinds of mental blocks are common and affect people in all spheres of life. Some so-called "learning disabilities" are actually a protective mindset interfering with and limiting certain kinds of thinking. After being shamed in a classroom, for example, someone might vow to *never speak in public.* So, their thinking gets muddled, and they can't find words whenever a teacher asks them a question. Just being in a classroom setting is enough to activate their mindset, which restricts their thinking.

In other cases, the mindset *over-focuses* the mind. For instance, someone may be attached to the concept that their *physical environment has to be clean.* They use their practical thinking, but their mindset narrows this practical thinking to one thing, *cleanliness.*

Another person may believe that a particular type of creativity will give them significance. The mindset might be: *I'm significant if I paint pictures.* This limits creative thinking; their mindset is only focused on painting pictures, so much of their creative thought processes remain untapped.

You can see how *emotional* decisions powerfully influence our minds. As long we cling to an idol to protect ourselves or to satisfy our hearts' needs, there will be a mindset distorting our thought processes. These mental fortifications will give way, however, with a proper heart attachment. To be sure, the clearest thinking people are those who cleave to God and experience His love. They are *emotionally* "rooted in love" and therefore, can *mentally* "comprehend" at a high level.

> **Ephesians 3:17-19:** *...so that Christ may dwell in your hearts through faith; and that you, **being rooted and grounded in love, may be able to comprehend** with all the saints what is the breadth and length and height and depth, and to know the love of Christ which surpasses knowledge, that you may be filled up to all the fullness of God. (emphasis added)*

Mindsets Deflect

Another terrible thing about a mindset is that it deflects the very thing that we long for and need. A mindset exists to make up for emotional wounds and deficits, yet it fails miserably at this job. In fact, it does the exact opposite; it deflects relational impartations that bring healing and restoration.

Someone may have an emotional deficit because they never experienced a father's acceptance or received fatherly impartations. So, they might have a mindset that says; *I have to perform to get fatherly approval.* This becomes their modus operandi with father figures and God. When a genuine father figure does come across their path, with *unconditional* acceptance, their mindset deflects this influence. Their mindset tells them they have to do something to get approval, so unconditional love simply doesn't compute.

Mindsets have specific criteria: *If I do X, I will get Y.* But, if Y comes along before there is an opportunity to do X, the mindset does not accept it. It deflects the good thing that comes without condition.

A young person may have a mindset that says, *I am not worthy of love unless I get "A"s on my report card.* When they receive a "B" in one class, they are devastated because they've not met their mindset's condition for deserving love. Even though the child's parents affirm and love them unconditionally, it has little effect. The child's mindset deflects love. Like a broken record, the same message plays over and over in their mind: *I'm only acceptable if I get "A"s.*

Mindsets even deflect the loving influence of God. They require us to do something to gain His acceptance. It takes *trust in Jesus* to give up on the work a mindset is demanding of us.

John 6:29: *Jesus answered and said to them, "This is the work of God, that you believe in Him whom He has sent."*

Projection

A mindset causes people to project what they believe to be true for themselves onto *others.* This kind of projection is common with parents. "I know what my kids are feeling and what they need," they say with confidence. But this can be the parent's mindset at work, painting a picture of what their kids are feeling and thinking.

Jean and I met a woman with an amazing knack for drawing out talents in people. Like a miner, she would find the hidden diamond, carve it out, dust it off, and polish it up. She had an incredible ability to identify a person's unique gifts. Of course, this strength of hers was also a liability. Bringing out the best in people became the all-important pursuit in her life; it became a mindset.

Her mindset projected onto her children. *My kids will be crushed if no one brings forth their unique gifts*, she thought. When one of her kids showed an interest in woodworking, she felt compelled to buy expensive tools. Another child said they wanted to play the piano, so she felt pressure to buy a top-of-the-line piano. She was convinced her children would feel devalued if their talents were not drawn out and activated. But this was *her* greatest fear. In reality, her children didn't see things the same way: they didn't value the same thing, fear the same thing, or feel the same urgency to do certain things.

Mindsets create a false paradigm about what's essential in life and what's necessary to maintain emotional security. But then they go a step further in projecting this view onto others. This projecting hurts relationships. Relationships require a listening ear, and an emotional faculty tuned into the feelings of others. But we can't do this when our mindset has us presuming to know what people are feeling and how they are processing things. Mindsets make it very difficult to be other-oriented; they keep us self-absorbed and isolated. When we look at things through the lens of a mindset, we can become an island unto ourselves, cut off from genuine relationships.

Actions Required by Mindsets

So far, we have talked about how protective mindsets affect our minds, how they restrict and narrow our thinking, and how they cause us to under-use or over-use certain kinds of thinking.

A mindset will affect behavior, as well, because it has a prescription for what we need to *do*. It pressures us to use some form of control, compliance, alignment, performance, or avoidance.

You could say mindsets get us into a state of fight or flight. But this is an oversimplification of their operations; they are much more sophisticated than a simple fight-or-flight mechanism.

MINDSETS

Mindsets vary as much as people do. One mindset can be all about *avoiding* certain kinds of people, while another requires the person to *find* a type of person.

Some mindsets require a rather simple action, like *achieve success*. Others are more complex, requiring the person to *search* for a specific type of person and then perform an action. For example, *find a father figure and serve him.*

A mindset may involve downright bizarre behavior. It might require a person to *use facial expressions to pacify "dangerous" people*, like authority figures. Without realizing it, the person is wearing a phony smile the minute a father figure walks into the room.

A mindset may also limit expressions. Someone might decide that it is *better to be seen and not heard*, so their mindset has them shutting down their speech.

Mindsets often require entirely irrational behavior. Even though a person never achieves a sense of wellbeing, their mindset has them doing the same senseless action and running into the same brick wall.

Sometimes, mindsets take people right into a den of lions. A woman who is emotionally damaged by an abusive father might marry an abusive man. Her mindset actually *seeks* an abuser. She may believe that if she can get an abusive man like her father to love her, it proves she's valuable.

Clearly, mindsets can be the source of delusional and dangerous behavior. We've seen people in relatively good marriages hook up with an extra-marital partner. Their mindset tells them if they can get a specific type of person to love them, they will no longer feel shame from their childhood. This kind of behavior is completely irrational, yet people have a strong compulsion to follow their mindset wherever it takes them.

Early in our marriage, Jean felt awkward in our relationship, not because I was abusive, but because I was *kind*. One day when I came home from work, she was vacuuming the house as if her life depended on it. When I asked her why she was so intense, she fired back, "I'm vacuuming to make you happy!" I said, "Well, that's nice, but I am already happy with you." She looked at me utterly mystified because it ran contrary to her mindset. Believe it or not, it took some time for her to feel comfortable with my kindness because her mindset was telling her to *find a disapproving man and please him.*

People are often drawn to one another because their dysfunctions pull together like magnets. Their mindsets work together. When one person believes they need to *control* people to avoid abandonment and another believes they need to *appease* to be loved, the two come together. But it is an unhealthy, dysfunctional union.

Even in healthy marriages, mindsets are often the primary source of conflict. Both husband and wife are looking through the eyes of their mindsets, wanting their spouse to fulfill specific criteria. Mindsets cause them to misinterpret the motives and genuine feelings of their spouse.

I remember a woman saying, "My husband is wonderful in many ways, but he doesn't *defend* me, so he doesn't love me." We pointed out that, by her admission, her husband loved her in many ways. But she still insisted he did not love her because he was not defending her. She couldn't see beyond the bounds of her defense mindset. Unfortunately, no amount of defending on the part of her husband or anyone else would satisfy her mindset's demands. The truth is, a mindset is never really satisfied.

It may be tempting to give in to the demands of a spouse's mindset; this may seem to be the "loving" thing to do. But mindsets, like other things the Bible mentions, never say "enough."

Proverbs 30:15b-16: There are three things that are never satisfied, four that never say, 'Enough!': the grave, the barren womb, land, which is never satisfied with water, and fire, which never says, 'Enough!' (NIV)

Giving in to the demands of someone's mindset never works. Ultimately, a mindset has to be uprooted by a renewal of heart and mind, by the working of the Holy Spirit.

Cyclical Relationships

Mindsets draw people into cyclical relationships. Unconsciously, their mindset has them partnering with a specific kind of person so they might "rewrite" their personal history.

For instance, if a woman didn't feel loved by her controlling father, she may seek love from a controlling man. So, her mindset might be: *Appease a controlling man so that he loves you.* The last thing she wants is to marry a controller, yet her mindset presses her to find a man like her father. It tells her that if she complies and appeases just right, the controller will love her. She wrongly believes that if she can get approval from *this type of person*, it will finally prove she has value. But it never works out that way. The men in her life often take advantage of her. To make matters worse, the controller may have a mindset that *seeks an appeaser*.

Two dysfunctional systems fit together like a hand in a glove.

Both the controller and appeaser reinforce each other's mindsets. So, they remain attached to their mindset, and in an unhealthy way, to one another, rather than the Lord.

Mindsets can draw in certain dysfunctional personalities. A negative belief about ourselves creates a kind of invisible current that can pull in the wrong types of people and their bad behaviors.

Cyclical Relationship Patterns

If we believe we do not have value, people tend to treat us as such. Unconsciously, they are responding to our belief system. It's like having a large sign hanging over us: "I don't have value, so go ahead, reject me."

When I was in pilot training, I experienced a lot of harsh treatment by instructors. No matter what I did, it seemed like I'd get a tongue lashing. At times, it was surreal to see how instructors, regardless of my performance, would verbally attack me. I recall an instructor gently telling my co-pilot, after he made several glaring mistakes in the simulator, "Everyone makes mistakes, don't worry about it." When it was my turn, and I made some insignificant errors, he said, with a blistering tone, "You're incompetent...you call yourself a captain?!"

At first, I thought this was simply the military-style training that was a part of the aviation culture. But I came to realize something else was going on. When my father was harsh with me as a child, I made a vow to *perform perfectly to avoid harsh treatment.* But this had the reverse effect; I drew in more harsh treatment. People felt justified in harshly correcting me for the slightest missteps; I seemed to be a magnet for harshness. Now, I'm not saying that my beliefs controlled people; these people were responsible for their behavior. My point is that my beliefs created a powerful current around me, and it was easier for some to jump into the flow and mistreat me. Thankfully, God healed my emotions in this area. He revealed, in various ways, His fatherly attributes to me, which restored my inner man. I can honestly say that my performance mindset is gone, and harshness doesn't follow me anymore.

Having my mind renewed also opened me up to deeper relationships because I was able to show more of my true self. A mindset is rooted in a lie that we are shameful and need to cover ourselves, so it has us presenting a false self that masks our true identity. When I was doing things to avoid harsh treatment, I wasn't showing my true self. My actions were all about self-protection, rather than *self-revelation.* The doors of my heart were firmly closed as I put on behaviors – *a false self* – to protect myself. People couldn't get to know me because I was hiding behind performance and pleasing.

Mindsets have us living a contradiction. We are doing something to be accepted and yet wanting to be unconditionally loved. We are presenting a false self but desiring to be known for who we really are. God wants us secure in His love rather than being dependent on the criteria of a mindset. When we truly know His love, we won't be tracking in two directions and will be able to say "yes" and "no" in a definitive way.

*James 5:12: But above all, my brethren, do not swear, either by heaven or by earth or with any other oath; but your **yes is to be yes, and your no, no**, so that you may not fall under judgment. (emphasis added)*

God can change us inwardly, so we are no longer slaves to a mindset. When this happens, we won't be searching for or attracting dysfunctional people, and we can be our authentic selves.

Physical Effects of Mindsets

The spirit, soul, and body are in tight alignment. What goes on in the soul can overlap into the respective part of the physical body. The condition and health of the emotional heart affect the physical heart.

A thought pattern of the mind eventually turns into a physical brain pattern. According to the Christian worldview, we are more than just a physical brain. We have a spiritual mind, a soul mind, and a physical mind - these three overlap.

What happens in the inner man tends to work its way into the outer man. To some extent, a healthy inner life translates into a healthy outer life. God nourishes the spirit, the spirit feeds the soul, and the soul feeds the body.

Mindsets disrupt the normal flow of things. They can cause a kind of discontinuity in the wiring of the soul, which affects the physical body.

I knew a woman who was having difficulty expressing her feelings. The Lord gave me a vision and word of knowledge (Acts 9:10, 1 Cor. 12: 8-10) about her heart being "pinched," indicating it was difficult for her to express emotions. At the time, I believed this was strictly an emotional issue, something in her soul. But within days, the woman was in the hospital with *physical* heart palpitations. A doctor found an issue with one of her heart valves and, in fact, used the very same word, "pinched" to describe her physical heart problem. It turns out a mindset was in play. Many years earlier, this woman determined, it was unsafe to reveal her emotions, and therefore, she would *limit her emotional expressions*. This mindset created a problem in her soul, which overlapped into her body. A disruption in her heart at the soul level eventually worked its way into her physical heart.

Another friend of ours lost physical sensations in her face. Her doctor couldn't find anything wrong, so she was left without any explanation for this strange numbness in her face. As we talked about her past, it became clear that she vowed to *limit expressions to feel safe*. More specifically, she vowed to restrict *facial* expressions. A mindset formed that shut down her facial expressions and eventually ended up cutting off physical sensations to her face.

Some folks suffer from lower back pain due to carrying an emotional load. They may have a mindset such as, *I have to support myself,* so they mainly bear their burdens alone. Carrying this emotional weight stresses their lower back in their *soul*. This stress in their soul, the immaterial and unseen part of their being, turns into a pain in their *physical* lower back, the material part of them.

Mindsets wreak havoc with the body in indirect ways, as well. Many people have muscle tension in the back, shoulders, and neck due to the strain that goes with keeping up with the demands of a mindset.

Physical ailments are sometimes a sign of something deeper going on in the soul. They are often an emotional sickness manifesting in the body. When we try to nourish our souls on something other than God, we are bound to take in all sorts of toxins. If we eat and drink of the Lord (John 6:35; John 4:14), we will experience health in our spirits, souls, and bodies.

Hiding Christ

Christ's nature coming through us is the greatest threat to the kingdom of darkness. With so much on the line, it's no wonder demonic spirits attack our identity. They try to get us to be self-protective so that we might hide the nature of Christ within us.

> ***Matthew 5:16:*** *In the same way, let **your light shine** before others, that they may see your good deeds and glorify your Father in heaven. (NIV – emphasis added)*

Demonic spirits understand that if they can hurt us emotionally, a mindset will likely set up in our soul. Mindsets rob us of our true identity and personhood; we become a kind of machine as we comply, control, perform, or adjust to people. Our true self is hidden behind all that we do in trying to follow the dictates of our mindset.

Mindsets have us putting on a false self, and this ultimately means people don't see *Christ's* nature. Each believer is part of the body of Christ and that unique part, that "living stone," can only be seen when we live from our genuine selves.

> ***1 Peter 2:5****: You also, as **living stones**, are being built up as a spiritual house for a holy priesthood, to offer up spiritual sacrifices acceptable to God through Jesus Christ. (emphasis added)*

When we attach to a mindset, we are essentially burying the treasure that God has deposited within us. We're not "showing forth" the nature of Christ.

*1 Peter 2:9: But ye are a chosen generation, a royal priesthood, an holy nation, a peculiar people; that ye should **shew forth** the praises of him who hath called you out of darkness into his marvelous light (KJV – emphasis added)*

The Greek word for "shew forth" means "to proclaim to those without what has taken place within."[21] But we are hindered from showing forth Christ's nature without if we have a mindset operating within.

God is serious about having His nature shine through us. With "reverence and fear," we are to "show the results" of Christ's nature having been formed in us.

*Philippians 2:12: Dear friends, you always followed my instructions when I was with you. And now that I am away, it is even more important. **Work hard to show the results of your salvation**, obeying God with deep **reverence and fear.** (NLT –emphasis added)*

It might seem like being a non-person, a kind of robot, would allow God to shine brightly through us. But when we hide, Christ is also hidden. This is why Satan tries to get us attached to a mindset; to bottle us up and to hold back our unique expression of Jesus.

God has a wonderful and mysterious transaction in mind. When we become one with the Bridegroom Jesus, we also become like Him. And then, amazingly, His nature flows through our unique personality. Becoming one with God also restores our souls, which removes the nest where demonic birds have made their home. This frees us to walk in our true identity and particular expression of Christ.

Case Study: "The Entrepreneur"

Charlie has always been a unique individual; he beats to his own drum. As a boy scout, he was never satisfied with what he was taught and always wanted to try a new approach. In Sunday school, much to the dismay of his teacher, Charlie disrupted the class with his endless questions. When he sang in the school choir, he strayed off in different directions and sang solos, frustrating the director. At home, creative ideas flowed out like a river; Charlie always had a new idea, a unique solution, for anything and everything.

One particular passion near and dear to his heart, which Charlie can never seem to stop talking about, is using creativity and innovation in business. His siblings roll their eyes at him, wondering why anyone his age would care to ramble on about such things. His father tells him that his ideas are fanciful and that he needs to grow up and keep his feet grounded in reality.

Charlie's father has a lot of emotional baggage when it comes to being an entrepreneur. He had a failed business venture that depleted his finances and forced the family out of their home. He is dead set against any self-employment, often remarking, "That crazy entrepreneur stint cost me dearly."

Since then, his father found a government job and confidently tells Charlie that a position in the public sector is everything a person could ever want. It provides safety, security, and an excellent pension. Year after year, he feeds Charlie the same, stern advice: "You need a solid education and a government job with good benefits."

Charlie pays an emotional price for his original thinking. He is often scorned for his ideas and is a target for ridicule, being labeled as having his "head in the clouds."

The criticisms, like poison, penetrate his identity. Charlie feels that people not only dislike his ideas but also disdain him as a person. He believes that his creativity, his original thinking, is a character defect, a flaw in his personality.

Enduring such shame is not an option for Charlie, so he decides to change his mode of operation to something more practical and down-to-earth. He vows to stay focused on things that are already established and to avoid creative ideas. A mindset develops that stifles creative, original ideas. Although he is by nature an out-of-the-box thinker, his mindset deactivates this part of his mind and narrows his thinking.

After college, following his father's advice, Charlie interviews for several government positions. But it feels like he's just going through the motions; this vocational path had little to do with his desires or his talents. He craves an opportunity to unleash his creative ideas and start his own business. But Charlie feels uneasy venturing out into anything on his own. He is heading down a similar road as his father and the same familiar, demonic spirits pressure him to give up his entrepreneurial calling.

For a while, Charlie takes the safe road and accepts a government job. But over time, frustration builds up. He has a deep desire to use his creative thinking and longs for the day when he can start a business of his own. But his thoughts get muddied whenever he contemplates moving in a new direction. His mind seems to go blank when he tries to conceptualize any new ideas.

Charlie is aware that something is not quite right in his thinking and even wonders if there is something physically wrong with his brain."Did I fall in the night and hit my head?" he sometimes wonders. But a protective mindset is at work, which formed when Charlie vowed to protect himself by not using creative thinking. His inability to think clearly is due to an agreement, an inner vow, he made in the past.

After five years of working as a clerk in a government office, Charlie finally reaches a boiling point. No longer able to grind it out in his job, he knows that something has to give. He seeks help from a life coach at his church. After giving him an aptitude test, she determines that Charlie has chosen a career path that is entirely ill-suited for his strength and natural abilities. The coach also finds that Charlie has been making life decisions based on a distorted self-image. So, she encourages him to take a spiritual approach, suggesting He seek God for answers.

As Charlie cries out to God for healing, things begin to change in his emotional life. He is deeply touched by God's heart toward him and realizes God values the person that he is. Charlie was designed to be an original and creative person; it is not a personality flaw.

Charlie finds the Genesis 1 account of creation to be particularly striking. He is amazed at how God spoke everything into existence. Something clicks in Charlie when he reads this verse:

Genesis 1:3: God saw all that He had made, and behold, it was very good. And there was evening and there was morning, the sixth day.

All that God created was good. Charlie was made in God's image and was meant to be a creative person. He was not born with a defect but with something good, a part of God's nature, that he is to bring forth and express.

The more Charlie gets to know God, the Creative Father, the more secure he becomes. He no longer needs to withhold his original ideas because he now knows that God delights in him. This internal change puts him on the career path that he has longed for, as he applies his creative genius in new business ventures.

CHAPTER SIX

STRENGTHS

Identifying a person's strength is key to understanding their inner world. There's an old saying: "all roads lead to Rome." Well, when it comes to personal identity, all roads lead to a person's strength.

On the positive side, our strength is where we are *gifted* and where our *passion* lies. But there is often a negative aspect of our strength. Typically, our strength is also how we *measure our worth*, where we are emotionally *wounded and shamed*, how we *defend* ourselves, and what we turn into an *idol*.

Talents and Abilities Associated with Strength

God has woven the strength of a person through their faculties. In this diagram, we see that the gift of *compassion* operates in all three of the compassionate person's faculties.

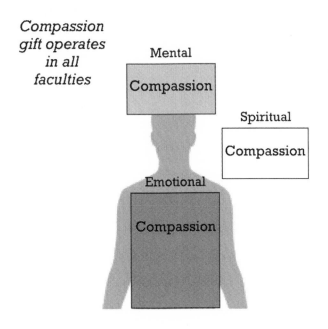

Compassion gift operates in all faculties

Mental

Compassion

Spiritual

Compassion

Emotional

Compassion

Firstly, this person has the *mental capacity* to use their gift of compassion; they *think* compassionately. Although compassion is more of an emotion-driven gift, the compassionate person still has an intellectual ability to use this strength. They see the needs of others and are keenly aware mentally of how and where to deliver their compassion.

Secondly, this strength is part of their *spiritual faculty*. They have a *sense* of when and to whom they are to administer their compassion. The Lord, who is full of compassion, also gives them guidance as to how to use their gift.

And, finally, this strength is incorporated into their *emotional faculty,* so they *feel* compassion for people. They also have an emotional value for compassion; in their view, it's what the world needs first and foremost.

God has given us unique talents that work in all three faculties so that we can help others.

Strength as Emotional Value

Values are a part of and flow from the emotional faculty. Some of these values are chosen, which is why the Bible tells us to "set our affection" in a direction.

> *Colossians 3:2: Set your affection on things above, not on things on the earth. (KJV - emphasis added)*

David made a conscious decision to set his affections on the Lord:

> *Psalm 16:8: I have set the LORD continually before me; Because He is at my right hand, I will not be shaken. (emphasis added)*

Although we have the flexibility to choose some of our values and where we set our affections, the value we have for our strength is hard-wired into our emotional faculty.

159

*Strength is a core value
at the center of the
emotional being*

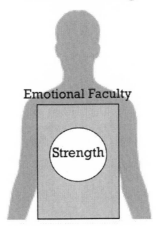

Because our strength is central to our identity and is so highly valued, it's tempting to become defined by it. We might think: *I'm using my strength and doing what's most important. Therefore, I am important.* But this is not true; our value is not based on what we do; we have *intrinsic* value.

God gave us a passion for using our strength so that we might be "Christ's body" (Rom. 12:5), helping others and showing God's nature.

Unfortunately, rather than focusing their strength outwardly to help others, many try to use it to gain inner security. Their strength effectively becomes an idol. They wrongly believe that if they use their strength well, it increases their value or significance.

Others make the mistake of using their strength to critique themselves. For instance, someone may have a knack for *understanding foundational and structural issues*. This ability to bring balance and find weak spots works well in developing a business or running an organization. Instead, they use this gift to find every little fault and weak point in their character and Christian walk.

Someone whose strength is *doing things with excellence* can become deeply discouraged when their life doesn't meet up to their standards. If they have any failures, it means they are not a person of excellence and therefore have no value.

There's a lie out there that says if we can get our strength firing on all four cylinders, we will feel secure. The life coach might jump in and say, "Wait a minute; we do need to maximize our potential and use all our God-given talents!" I agree this is important. But using our gifts can never bring emotional security.

The great challenge for all of us is differentiating between the importance of the strength and being defined by it. Although our strength is a part of our identity, and it will always be important to us, it does not ultimately define us. We are made in the image of God and, as Christians, are part of the family of God. Jesus paid an infinite price for us. This means we have infinite value, whether we are using our strength or not. These are essential Biblical truths to keep in mind when we are tempted to earn our value by using our strength.

Because our strength is woven into our identity, at some point we will come face-to-face with what it means to us and how we will use it. If we dethrone our strength and attach to God, we will understand at an emotional level that our value is intrinsic and will no longer be tempted to make our strength an idol.

Strength as "Love Language"

The strength of a person is also their love language. When leaders are led well, they also feel loved. When a compassionate person is given compassion, they feel loved. Because they value their strength the most, it makes sense that a person feels loved when they receive it.

Even if the leader is showered with another attribute, like compassion, it's not as meaningful. When it comes to love languages, the strength is the emotional sweet spot.

I remember one woman who loved *giving gifts*. She spent countless hours thinking about what people would like so she could give them an appropriate gift. After finding the perfect gift, she would search for a suitable accompanying card and write a carefully crafted, personalized note. Finally, she would pristinely package the gift. I commented that if giving gifts was her strength and a value to her, *receiving* gifts would also be important to her. She said, emphatically, "No, I like to give gifts. I don't care to receive them." When I asked her what it felt like to receive gifts, she said through a frown, "I hate to receive gifts because the minute I look at the package, it just feels so wrong. No one takes the time to figure out what's right for me and consider what I want." In reality, she greatly valued receiving gifts and was hurt when others didn't give with the same care and attention to detail. Her strength was indeed her love language.

Self-Protection and the Strength

It should come as no surprise that many of us fall back on our strength to protect us. It is tempting to use our strength to

162

counteract feelings of shame because we feel more valuable when our talents are in operation.

Let's take an example of a compassionate person who is reaching out to the poor and needy in the inner city. Her gift of compassion operates in all three faculties – thinking, sensing, and feeling – so she's fully equipped by God to fulfill this mission.

Initially, she uses her gift of compassion wisely and at the Holy Spirit's prompting. But what happens when this compassion-driven person gets emotionally wounded? She looks to her strength for protection. *I will give compassion to prove I'm valuable*, she vows. After having agreed to these terms, a compassion mindset develops.

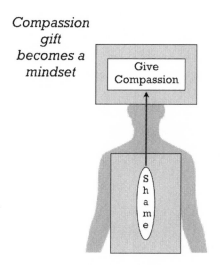

Compassion gift becomes a mindset

Give Compassion

Shame

Now she's in what seems to be a life-or-death struggle for internal security. Her compassion mindset is relentless in its demands. Like a cruel taskmaster, it requires strict obedience;

compassion must be given, or she has no value. She feels the need to give time, money, and emotional support to every needy person, all the time. Her compassion mindset doesn't allow her any freedom to say "no" or to limit her outflow, so she gives away all her resources.

She is double-minded. On one level, she desires to help people and knows that God has called her to give sacrificially. But there's also self-interest in what she does; she is using compassion to fight off shame. So, her strength is being used for both healthy and unhealthy reasons. It's a confusing situation where clear thinking and dysfunctional thinking, and good and bad motives, are at work in her soul.

It is impossible to measure up to any mindset's criteria. There's often a day of reckoning, an emotional crisis when a person sees that they can't meet up to their mindset's requirements. Some people run out of energy after years of striving and realize the futility of what they are doing. Yet, they still feel compelled to stay the course and comply with their mindset.

Mindsets follow this equation: *If you do X, you will get Y.* If you *give compassion, you are valuable.* The person agrees to be under a "law," which they must fulfill to be acceptable. Whenever we follow a law to gain righteousness, value, or acceptance, that law will accuse and condemn us.[22]

Romans 3:20: *because by the works of the Law no flesh will be justified in His sight; for* **through the Law comes the knowledge of sin.** *(emphasis added)*

When a person believes they *must be compassionate to be valuable*, they agree to meet the standards of the law of compassion. But they cannot possibly meet the requirements of this law. By faith, we trust that Christ Jesus has met the standards of the law, so we no longer have to do the works – the works of our strength – to be righteous.

*Galatians 3:11: Now that **no one is justified by the Law** before God is evident; for, "THE RIGHTEOUS MAN SHALL LIVE BY FAITH." (emphasis added)*

We can't use our strength to gain acceptance or prove we have value as a person. Christ's fulfillment of all the requirements of the law settled the issue.

*Galatians 2:16: nevertheless knowing that a man is not justified by the works of the Law but through faith in Christ Jesus, even we have believed in Christ Jesus, so that we may be **justified by faith in Christ** and **not by the works of the Law**; since by the works of the Law no flesh will be justified. (emphasis added)*

We have a heart attachment to our mindset. In a sense, we are "married" to it, and believe we have to follow its requirements. It's a law that we have embraced as a kind of savior and "husband." When the Apostle Paul is speaking about "dying to the law," he uses an analogy of a husband dying and the wife being free to remarry. Similarly, we are no longer to be "married to the law," the requirements of a mindset, but to Christ Jesus.

*Romans 7:4: Therefore, my brethren, you also were made to **die to the Law through the body of Christ, so that you might be joined to another**, to Him who was raised from the dead, in order that we might bear fruit for God. (emphasis added)*

165

There's a beautiful bridal paradigm here. We are to be "joined" to the Bridegroom; this is how our soul gets life and how we "bear fruit."

Yes, we are to be good stewards of our gifts, and God will require us to use our unique strength. And He will hold us accountable for how we use our talents (Luke 12:48). That being said, God wants to meet our hearts' needs through a relationship with Himself. He is jealous to do this and often undercuts our attempts to use our strength to find value or to self-protect. *He is our security; our strength is not.*

Unhealthy use of the strength is self-focused and invariably gets us into striving. This a red flag that the strength is being used for the wrong purposes, and we are being defined by our strength. Healthy use of the strength is focused outward, glorifies God, and has an "easy yoke."

> **Matthew 11:30:** *"For My yoke is easy and My burden is light."*

Strength as a Character Quality of Christ

God has designed people with unique strengths to serve others. A believer, operating in their strength, is God's hands and feet to the world. They are Christ's "body."

> **1 Corinthians 12:12:** *For even as the body is one and yet has many members, and all the members of the body, though they are many, are one body, so also is Christ.*

Our strength has an outward functionality, but at the same time, it is to be part of our nature. God wants to work within, with our character, and then move to the externals, to our works. What does this mean? We are not only to functionally use our strength, but we are to "become" our strength, so it is part of our nature and character.

I know one woman whose talents and nature flow together beautifully. She's able to bring peace outwardly with her negotiation skills. But this is not what stands out about her. She emits peace from within; it flows from her inner being. She was forever changed when God gave her peace to get through some terrible situations. She had a personal encounter with the God of peace (Rom.15:33). When this happened, God deposited part of His nature – *His peace* – into her. Because of this divine deposit, calm and tranquility seem to ooze out of her pores. This character trait of Christ has become part of her character. When you are in her presence, no words are necessary; you feel peace.

When we have the character of our strength, we become a "letter of Christ," and others come in contact with a unique aspect of Jesus' nature. In essence, they are "reading" something about Jesus that is within us.

*2 Corinthians 3:2-3: You are our letter, written in our hearts, known and **read** by all men; being manifested that you are a **letter of Christ**, cared for by us, written not with ink but with the Spirit of the living God, not on tablets of stone but on **tablets of human hearts.** (emphasis added)*

But often our inner life doesn't parallel our outer life. The story of Elijah is a testimony to the fact that outward acts of the strength do not necessarily reflect the stature of the inner man. If ever there was a person with raw courage, zealousness, and faith, it was Elijah. He fearlessly took on false prophets, and God backed up his courageous faith with unbelievable signs and wonders (1 Kings 18:17-46). But Elijah fell into a trap that is all-too-common for most of us: he became dependent on his strength. He trusted in his own courage and on his own faith. He became focused on the mighty works of God rather than God Himself. When Elijah didn't get the results he wanted, he became deeply discouraged. I imagine him thinking: *I don't see other prophets of God displaying mighty works...If I can't change things with the awesome power that surrounds my life, there's no hope!* After confronting hundreds of false prophets, he found himself depressed and vulnerable to the threat of one woman, Jezebel.

God then did something internal with Elijah. He unveiled His greatness in a way different from the dramatic outward signs Elijah was accustomed to seeing. God revealed Himself in a "still small voice."

> ***1 Kings 19:11-13:*** *And he said, "Go forth, and stand upon the mount before the LORD." And, behold, the LORD passed by, and a great and strong wind rent the mountains, and brake in pieces the rocks before the LORD; but the LORD was not in the wind. And after the wind an earthquake; but the LORD was not in the earthquake. And after the earthquake a fire; but the LORD was not in the fire. And after the fire a **still small voice**. And it was so, when Elijah heard it, **that he wrapped his face in his mantle**..." (KJV - emphasis added)*

Wrapping his face in his mantle was an act of extreme reverence. The eyes of Elijah's heart opened, and he understood God in a way that far exceeded what he knew of Him through outward signs and wonders. Elijah was completely awe-struck by God's nature. Through this face-to-face-encounter, he went from beholding God's awesome acts to beholding (2 Cor. 3:18) the God *who is awesome.* He communed with the One who is majestic and holy beyond description.

I believe this had a profound effect on Elijah. After coming in contact with God's essence and character, something shifted internally. Elijah's strength was matured; it became a part of his character. You could say, Elijah *became* his strength. So, he was no longer just a man doing mighty works; He became a mighty man of God.

Using our talents and abilities comes easily, but the internal transformation, where the maturity and character of the strength are developed, is often a struggle. We have to allow God to overcome our strength for it to be perfected, which requires laying down our strength and all that it means to us.

We all need to let go of our strength as a form of security – as a false husband – and embrace our true Husband, Jesus.

2 Corinthians 11:2: *For I am jealous for you with a godly jealousy; for I betrothed you to* **one husband***, so that to Christ I might present you as a pure virgin. (emphasis added)*

Union with the Bridegroom allows us to reflect the character of Christ Jesus, not just in what we do, but who we are.

Case Study: "The Atmosphere-Changing Woman"

Sara has a presence, a unique, intangible quality that people pick up on the minute she walks into a room. Without saying or doing anything, she changes the atmosphere and lifts people's spirits.

When Sara reads books about personality types, she can't find anything that remotely describes her traits. Her strength is unusual and difficult to define because it springs from within. She is a rare, often misunderstood type. You might say Sara is more a "be"er than a "do"er.

Even in her stillness and quietness, Sara powerfully affects people. They sense something radiating from her. Security seems to emit from her, so they enjoy just sitting in her presence and looking into her reassuring eyes.

Sara's nature is similar to her mother's, who also exudes a presence, a sort of fragrance that permeates a room and requires few words. Her father, on the other hand, is an intellectual genius, an engineer by trade. He carefully thinks through every concept and then masterfully uses the English language to express his complex thoughts.

Unfortunately, Sara's father uses his superior intellect and precise words to carve up his children. Every meal becomes a debate where Sara's older brothers and sisters go head-to-head with their father. The children leave the table emotionally bruised after being criticized and belittled each time they dared to speak a word or share a thought.

Sara makes no effort to keep up with her father's intellect and does everything she can to hide from his daily tirades. Interestingly, her father seldom takes aim at her, knowing somehow this would not be fitting for his youngest daughter's quiet dignity.

But the damage is done. The constant criticisms and volatility, though not directed at Sara, affect her sensitive soul. During these turbulent childhood years, Sara makes determinations about her value. She feels shame about her introverted personality, believing that her inability to verbally joust is a personality flaw. Because Sara has no hope of compensating for this "defect" by becoming quick on her feet verbally, she vows to never draw attention to herself. If any authority figures come across her path, she will shift the focus off of herself and onto them. And then before they get a chance to attack and demean her, she will quickly figure out a way to appease them.

A mindset develops in Sara's thinking that has her continuously monitoring authorities; she's ever alert to their words, facial expressions, and tones. This mindset doesn't allow her any room to be herself or have any attention drawn to herself; it keeps her hidden away. Life is all about protecting herself from criticism, from a father figure devaluing and demeaning her.

After struggling for years, Sara's life is profoundly changed when she meets God. She begins to find the security that had been missing for so long through a relationship with Jesus. Sara begins a step-by-step process with the Holy Spirit of renewing her emotions and mind. Her old patterns and mindsets don't give way immediately, but she takes comfort in the fact that the renewal of her soul is progressive.

2 Corinthians 4:16: Therefore, we do not lose heart, but though our outer man is decaying, yet our inner man is being renewed day by day.

Colossians 3:10: ...and have put on the new self who is being renewed to a true knowledge according to the image of the One who created him.

As Sara submits herself to her Heavenly Father and trusts Him with the most vulnerable places of her heart, things change in her soul. The mindset that caused her to hide gives way as she becomes more attached to God. She encounters a God who, unlike her father, is secure. Sara doesn't have to worry about God suddenly blowing up or being hot-tempered. There's no need to monitor His actions carefully. In fact, God is so secure that He will give her time and attention. He doesn't want Sara to hide but wants her to come forth as a unique individual.

Sara finds that an intimate connection with God gives her the security to be the person she was created to be. She comes to realize that her inner qualities are "precious in God's sight" (1 Pet. 3:4) and her greatest strength.

CHAPTER SEVEN

IDOLS

man's nature, so to speak, is a perpetual factory of idols

~John Calvin

The term "idol" may bring to mind the Israelites bowing down to the golden calf in the book of Exodus, but idolatry has more to do with trusting something or someone other than God to meet our heart needs. I've divided these "heart needs" into five categories: safety, security, sanctification, significance and satisfaction. Most idolatry comes from trying to meet these basic emotional needs apart from God.

Idols can be things, people, or concepts. We might trust in *a job to feel significant,* a *spouse to feel secure,* or the *idea of unity to feel safe.*

The things we do to feel secure can be idols, such as: *plan, build, perform, appease, create,* or *control.* Or, idols may involve not doing things like: *not speaking, not creating, not hoping,* or *not participating.*

Idols can be ideologies passed down from one generation to another, such as: we are *significant if we are intelligent, valuable if we are a professional,* or *safe if we stick together.* Or, they can be broad-sweeping ideologies like: *life is hopeless, so don't dream,* or, *God won't help us, so we have to make our own way.*

There are idols we use to try to cleanse our consciences and make us feel righteous, including various *religious rituals, traditions, or good works.*

We might turn material possessions into an idol when we look to them for satisfaction. Although we may get some satisfaction through material things, they won't meet our ultimate need for satisfaction.

When it comes to our heart needs, there's no in-between. If we don't have a functioning relationship with God, where He meets these needs, we will search for an idol to make up the deficit. What we do with our soul's hunger and thirst, where we eat and drink, is the most critical decision we make in this life.

Many Christians don't realize how powerful this inner drive is to find nourishment for their souls. They deal mainly with the externals, how to have a victorious Christian life, and they primarily look to God for blessings or a helpful hand in times of crisis. Meanwhile, deep within, their souls thirst for something more, for a drink from the living God.

> **Psalm 42:1b:** *As the deer pants for the water brooks, so my soul pants for You, O God.*

If our soul is hungry, and we don't eat of God, there's a tendency to look for an idol. This temptation goes back to the Garden of Eden when God gave man "every tree that is pleasing to the sight and good for food."

> **Genesis 2:9:** *Out of the ground the LORD God caused to grow every tree that **is pleasing to the sight** and **good***

for food; the tree of life also in the midst of the garden...*(emphasis added)*

Satan came to Eve with a twist. He appealed to her appetites, also telling her she could have *fruit that was good for food* and a *delight to the eyes*, but with one difference: Satan tempted her with *knowledge*. He promised her that she would be like God, and her desires would be met apart from Him.

Genesis 3:6: *When the woman saw that the tree was* **good for food,** *and that it was a* **delight to the eyes,** *and that the tree was desirable to* **make one wise**, *she took from its fruit and ate; and she gave also to her husband with her, and he ate. (emphasis added)*

There were two offers. God's offer was life and fulfillment through *knowledge of Himself.* Satan's offer was life and satisfaction in *being knowledgeable and God-like*; the *idol of knowledge.*

God was offering Adam and Eve things that would satisfy them. There was nothing wrong with having hunger; it was God-given. However, this hunger was meant to drive them toward God, which is why He made mention of something significant: *the tree of life.* This tree represented God's person, His nature. Experiencing the excellencies of His person would be their source of life. In the New Testament, this is made abundantly clear.

John 17:3: Now this is eternal life: that they know *[ginóskó - experiential knowing] you, the only true God, and Jesus Christ, whom you have sent. (NIV - emphasis, brackets added)*

By eating from the tree of life, their souls would be nourished. Adam and Eve had the opportunity to eat of God's nature by walking and talking with Him, fellowshipping with Him. Life would come from being in contact with His beautiful person; this would satisfy their soul hunger.

But Adam and Eve took Satan's offer when they ate from the tree of knowledge of good and evil. They made knowledge and wisdom an idol and looked to it for heart security and significance.

Adam and Eve's story sheds light on the fact we all have heart hunger. Satan tries to deceive and lead us astray in the area of devotion. He knows that what we worship and are devoted to, we will also eat from and get our nourishment.

*2 **Corinthians** 11:3: But I am afraid that, as the serpent deceived Eve by his craftiness, your minds will be led astray from the simplicity and purity of devotion to Christ.*

As the apostle Paul points out, Satan is "crafty" in his tactics. He doesn't necessarily tempt people to go after evil things, but lesser things. Eve was tempted by something that looked good to her and was deceived into believing that ultimate satisfaction could come from good things, minus God.

Adam and Eve's fall was more than just an act of disobedience. Although it was that, it was also a heart decision to worship an idol. They chose where they would direct their devotion and where they were going to be nourished.

We need to trust in God's character and kind intentions toward us. He will fulfill our longings and satisfy our hearts. Most Christians aren't trying to get satisfied by sinful behavior or a walk on the dark side but are trying to squeeze fulfillment and ultimate meaning out of good things. Elevating good things to idol status is a subtle and enticing trap. But when we aim low, we miss the tree of life and the heavenly prize.

Aim at Heaven and you will get Earth 'thrown in';

aim at Earth and you will get neither

~ C.S. Lewis [23]

Mindsets Are Idols

I vividly remember the day when I realized mindsets are idols. We were ministering to a gentleman who had a way of deflecting everything we said, especially if we discussed his inner life. Every time we tried to address an issue, he countered with a quick-witted comment. *Humor* was his source of protection; it was his mindset. We wanted to laugh along with him as it all seemed so light-hearted and fun. But at the same time, we knew we were running directly into a fortress of self-protection.

The following day I spoke with him, and his demeanor was completely different. With sober words, he described how the Holy Spirit had highlighted the following Bible text:

1 Samuel 12:21: Do not turn away after useless idols. They can do you no good, nor can they rescue you, because they are useless. (NIV)

God made it clear to him that his self-protective mindset was an idol. He realized that his humor, which seemed so innocent, was just as serious to God as any other type of idol worship. His

177

horsing around had become his functional god; a god he depended on to protect himself from shame.

Once our trust is placed in something for emotional security, whether it is humor or some other solution, a mindset forms. And that mindset effectively becomes our idol.

Emotional trauma makes us particularly vulnerable to idolatry. The feeling of shame is so devaluing and visceral that we feel pressed for an instant remedy. Before we know it, we are agreeing to a solution that can't help us and actually works against us.

A mindset, like any idol, pressures us. It demands certain things of us and promises heart security if we fulfill our end of the bargain. But this is a deal with the devil. When we don't give the idol what it wants, there's a backlash: fear, insecurity, and shame come at us with a vengeance.

For example, a person might have a mindset that requires them to do everything perfectly. They have trusted perfectionism as a way to fight off feelings of shame and to essentially prove their value as a person. But when they don't measure up to their mindset's standards, they feel even worse about themselves. In a twisted way, they have proven that they do not have value when they fail to meet their mindset's requirements. So, their feelings of shame intensify.

Our mindsets don't help us and, in fact, end up torturing us. But that's because our mindsets are idols, and idols always fail us. If we trust in them, our souls can't hold onto security; we resemble leaky "cisterns."

> ***Jeremiah 2:13:*** *My people have committed two sins: They have forsaken me, the spring of living water, and have dug their own cisterns, broken cisterns that cannot hold water. (NIV)*

178

When we understand that our mindsets are idols, the path of restoration and renewal becomes clear. We need to shift our *heart* attachments to God and trust Him to fulfill our ultimate need for significance, satisfaction, security, safety, and sanctification.

A mindset cannot be overcome by forcing ourselves to think differently or by behavior modification. We need the bottom-up approach, where we *from the heart* forsake the mindset and all that it means to us. If we embrace God and look to Him to meet our needs, He will become the "spring of living water" within us.

Safety Idols

One of the heart needs is for safety, both *physical* and *emotional*. In the Old Testament, Israel was in covenant with God, as a wife to a husband. God was Israel's protective husband, the "Lord of Hosts."

> **Isaiah 54:5:** *"For your **husband** is your Maker, whose name is the **LORD of hosts**; And your Redeemer is the Holy One of Israel, who is called the God of all the earth. (emphasis added)*

But Israel shifted her trust to other nations, seeking idols for safety. King Ahaz feared for his and Judah's safety and thus became unfaithful to the Lord. He asked for the support from an enemy nation, Assyria (2 Chron. 28:16). And then King Ahaz "in time of distress," went further into darkness as he sacrificed to the "gods of Aram" for protection (2 Chron. 28:22-23).

Had Israel remained in a relationship with God, her spiritual Husband, *He* would have met her need for safety.

We, much like ancient Israel, may trust in idols when we feel like our safety is in question. This might mean trusting in a union job or the government, or, for the rich, it may mean clinging to money for safety.

Proverbs 18:11: *A rich man's wealth is his strong city, and like a high wall in his own imagination.*

Some believe an alignment with a family member, a boss, or an authority figure, will provide them with a protective covering. Those who grow up with absentee fathers are often tempted to find a safety idol. They can become overly dependent on someone like a pastor, as their ultimate protector. While a pastor may provide some protection, they can't fully meet this deep-seated need for safety.

Emotional safety played a role in dozens of aviation accidents in the 1970s. Airplanes ran out of gas, fell out of the sky, crashed into each other, and exploded into mountains. These tragedies were not due to unsafe planes but emotionally unsafe cockpits, where the communication broke down between the crew members. At that time, the captain was a god-like figure, never to be questioned. When the captain didn't have the aircraft properly configured, or if he misunderstood an air controller's instructions, the co-pilot was afraid to speak up. In several instances, a co-pilot allowed an airplane to crash rather than say something. Quite simply, the co-pilot didn't feel emotionally safe. In fact, neither the captain nor co-pilot felt safe emotionally. The captain felt disrespected and emotionally unsafe if he was questioned or corrected. The co-pilot feared a verbal attack and being demeaned personally (and he often was), so he kept his mouth shut. A dramatic change came when the concept of Crew Resource Management (CRM) was introduced to the aviation industry. CRM taught captains and co-pilots to work together as a team, but more importantly, it helped create an emotionally safe environment in the cockpit. This largely reduced accidents.

When we feel unsafe, there's a tendency to close ourselves off emotionally. And when we close the door to our emotions, we don't share or express ourselves. It also prevents us from experiencing God's protective and peaceful nature. Trusting and being vulnerable with God are keys to inwardly experiencing safety, as well as God's other attributes.

Shame also makes us feel unsafe emotionally. For many, the thought of re-experiencing shame is like facing a firing squad; it's terrifying. So, it's tempting to trust in a safety idol. A person may experience shame because they are verbally attacked and put down. They then attach to a safety idol like *people-pleasing*, where they do everything possible to align themselves with influential people, much like King Ahaz did when he tried to get help from the kings of Assyria.

Because shame makes us feel unworthy of God's protection, it makes it hard to believe that He will, or even wants to, protect us. So, we look elsewhere.

God offers us a spousal-type union with Himself. Because He is our spiritual Husband, we can trust Him. When we open ourselves to God emotionally, we experience the covenant relationship and come to know Him inwardly as the *protective* Husband.

Micah prophesied of "this one," Jesus, who would "be our peace."

*Micah 5:5: **This One will be our peace**. When the Assyrian invades our land, When he tramples on our citadels, Then we will raise against him Seven shepherds and eight leaders of men. (emphasis added)*

181

God doesn't necessarily protect us from all outside influences. He doesn't always create tranquil situations in our lives or rain down peace upon us. Instead, He gives Himself as the Bridegroom, the Husband, who *is* peace.

Ephesians 2:14a: *For He Himself is our peace.*

Security Idols

We all need to know that we are loved; we need to be *secure* in love. Security is often missing when love has not been experienced. Because this kind of knowing anchors the soul, the Apostle Paul prays for the experience of God's love. He wants us to have personal contact with Jesus, as this is the way we become "filled" with Him and secure in love.

> ***Ephesians 3:19:*** *...and to **know [ginóskó – experiential knowing] the love of Christ** which surpasses knowledge, that you may be **filled up to all the fullness of God**. (emphasis, brackets added)*

Without this experience, our hearts tend to stray from Him and look for security idols.

Security idols may come in the form of human relationships: parents, spouses, children, or friends.

Obviously, these relationships serve a purpose and are ordained by God so that we might experience love. They serve as a foundation from which we develop our relationship with Him. But when we look to humans to meet our *ultimate* needs of security, we quickly get into trouble. When we press people to love us and meet our security needs, we end up starving the relationships of oxygen. This kind of setup, where someone gives in the hope that love is reciprocated, never works.

Trying to get too much from people can lead to dysfunctional partnerships. Instead of two getting to know one another, there's a quid pro quo: *I'll give you something if you give me something.* People often end up in co-dependent relationships because they feel they need each other for security. Relationships, quite simply, do not work that way. Healthy relationships, where we experience another person, require an open-handedness. When people feel coerced, they quickly close the doors to their emotions and shut people out.

I recall a woman being quite upset by the fact that her husband wouldn't "open up" to her. She expected him to share his feelings and then listen intently to what she had to say. Although this sounded like a reasonable request, in reality, she was trying to get security by having what *looked like* a functional relationship. Her insistence on intimate conversations had the opposite effect; her husband pulled farther and farther away. He sensed that she really wasn't interested in getting to know him. She effectively made the functionality of the relationship a security idol. Ironically, if her focus had been on getting to know her husband, without any demands, she might have experienced more security.

This is true of God, as well. If we make knowing Him the ends, rather than a means to an end, we will experience His loving nature and become more secure in love.

Sanctification Idols

We all have a conscience that tells us right from wrong and a desire to be righteous. Because we are made in the image of God, and He is holy, there's an innate drive for holiness within us. We crave a feeling of being morally clean, of being *sanctified*.

If this heart-motivation is not met *in Christ*, we tend to look to sanctification idols, "dead works," to cleanse our consciences.

Hebrews 9:14: *...how much more will the blood of Christ, who through the eternal Spirit offered Himself without blemish to God, cleanse your conscience from dead works to serve the living God?*

These dead works come in many forms. Some try to satisfy the sanctification-longing by performing religious rituals or doing good works. Christians may strive to follow the Ten Commandments, or even the Mosaic Law, as a way to feel righteous and purified.

Rather than cleansing ourselves by doing something, like eating certain foods, we need our hearts to be "strengthened by grace."

Hebrews 13:9: *Do not be carried away by varied and strange teachings; for it is good for **the heart to be strengthened by grace**, **not by foods**, through which those who were so occupied were not benefited. (emphasis added)*

The drive for sanctification is in play with the non-Christian, as well. Most religions require good works and sacrifice for purification. And everyone, whether they believe in God or not, wants to be sanctified.

People may give money, volunteer, or become politically active to feel righteous. Others focus on healthy eating or exercise as a way to feel inwardly pure. Some people go to great lengths to keep their physical bodies clean to purify their consciences. I knew a young lady who would take a shower when she felt morally impure.

She believed, in a strange way, that if her body were clean, she would feel pure in her soul. Needless to say, this outward act didn't give her a feeling of being inwardly washed.

Similarly, some try to keep their physical environment, their home and office, spotless. They strive to keep everything tidy, picked up, and polished, in hopes that it will satisfy their heart need for sanctification.

However, outward acts never satisfy the need for a cleansing of the inner man. Even when Israel was under the Old Covenant, their consciences were not cleansed through the animal sacrifices. The sacrifices and the earthly tabernacle were just a symbol of what was to come in Christ.

Hebrews 9:9: ...which is a symbol for the present time. Accordingly, both gifts and sacrifices are offered which cannot make the worshiper perfect in conscience.

Following the Law didn't cleanse or make a person "perfect." The unclean feelings and the consciousness of sin persisted.

Hebrews 10:10: For the Law, since it has only a shadow of the good things to come and not the very form of things, can never, by the same sacrifices which they offer continually year by year, make perfect those who draw near. Otherwise, would they not have ceased to be offered, because the worshipers, having once been cleansed, would no longer have had consciousness of sins?

Shame intensifies our feelings of impurity and tends to drive us to a sanctification idol and self-cleansing. Conviction, on the other hand, draws us to God, to depend on His cleansing work.

Feeling convicted by the Holy Spirit for doing something wrong or failing to live a holy life, is a good thing. It propels us to seek forgiveness, restoration, and cleansing from God. Conviction points people to God for purification, rather than to an idol.

But shame has quite the opposite effect. It makes people want to flee from God and cling to a sanctification idol. Maybe they go overboard in religious works and spiritual activities, rather than repenting and trusting in Jesus' righteousness.

Shame keeps us self-focused, isolated, and without hope. If we turn our backs on it and face the Lord, He has a way of challenging its message and removing it from our souls. We still need to go through God's process of conviction, repentance, and cleansing, but without shame pointing its condemning finger at us.

Although everyone has a natural desire to feel cleansed, some personality types have an extra drive toward righteousness, purity, and holiness. Those with a prophetic calling (Eph. 4:11; 1 Cor. 12:28) have a built-in motivation to promote holiness. Being clean and holy is a core value for these folks. Because prophetic people have an acutely sensitive conscience, they need, more than any other personality type, to have a clear understanding that their righteousness is "not their own."

*Philippians 3:9: ...and may be found in Him, **not having a righteousness of my own** derived from the Law, but that which is through faith in Christ, the righteousness which comes from God on the basis of faith (emphasis added)*

If they don't get this straight, they become especially vulnerable to sanctification idols. They might go overboard with good works and striving to please God. Or they may become so discouraged and condemned about their uncleanliness that they say, "Who cares?" and get into a pattern of sin. They need to first look to the perfect One for their righteousness, and then their works will be properly motivated.

This brings up some crucial points. Firstly, in God's eyes, we are not morally clean; we are fallen beings who fall short of His glory (Rom. 3:23).

Secondly, we can't make up for this righteousness deficit through works. Doing good deeds is never going to make us pure in God's eyes or satisfy our longing to be sanctified.

Thirdly, even though we are not pure, God loves us and made us with infinite value. Jesus died for us while we were sinners (Rom. 5:8). He loves us in spite of our impurity. God calls us out as impure (Rom. 3:20), yet lovingly provides a way of cleansing (Rom. 7:25). Such is the nature of godly conviction; it causes us to feel bad for our sinfulness, yet draws us to God for cleansing.

Shame, on the other hand, tells us we are unredeemable, and it diminishes God's power and His goodness. Shame pushes us to take things into our own hands and tempts us to go to a sanctification idol for help.

Conviction brings "godly sorrow," which leads to "repentance," turning toward God, and results in "salvation." But shame brings "worldly sorrow" that leads to "death."

2 Corinthians 7:10: For the sorrow that is according to the will of God produces a repentance without regret, leading to salvation, but the sorrow of the world produces death.

Shame makes us want to cover our sin, as Adam and Eve, when they sewed leaves to cover themselves. It keeps us focused on ourselves and how bad we are, rather than God's mercy and His ability and willingness to cleanse us.

Consider how differently Peter and Judas responded to the Lord after they betrayed Him. Peter was convicted of his sin, became sorrowful in a Godly way, and was cleansed. Judas embraced shame, was sorrowful in a worldly way, and died with blood-stained hands.

If we embrace shame and accept its message as true, we will be tempted to look at what we can do to establish our own righteousness, which is "being ignorant of God's righteousness."

Romans 10:3: *For they being ignorant of God's righteousness, and going about to establish their own righteousness, have not submitted themselves unto the righteousness of God. (KJV)*

None of us are righteous based on our works (Rom. 3:20), but we can obtain *God's* righteousness *by faith* in Jesus Christ (Gal. 2:16). Our works are essential to God, but the minute we think our good deeds make us righteous, or that we can walk holy lives apart from God's grace (Titus 2:11-12), we are on a slippery slope. We will find ourselves clinging to an idol.

The only way to truly experience cleansing is to trust in God's righteousness and sanctification through Christ. The author of Hebrews urges us to "rest" from our works. We are to trust in what God has done in His "finished work."

Hebrews 4:1-3: *Therefore, let us fear if, while a promise remains of entering His rest, any one of you may seem to have come short of it. For indeed we have had good news preached to us, just as they also; but the word they heard did not profit them, because it was not united by faith in those who heard. For* **we who have believed enter that rest,** *just as He has said, "AS I SWORE IN MY WRATH, THEY SHALL NOT ENTER MY REST," although*

His works were finished from the foundation of the world. (emphasis added)

God alone gives us real cleansing; one which makes us "whiter than snow."

Psalm 51:7: Purify me with hyssop, and I shall be clean; Wash me, and I shall be whiter than snow.

Significance Idols

We all need to feel we have significance and have something valuable to contribute to the world. This heart-motivation for meaning is found in everyone, whether they believe in God or are an atheist.

There's a tricky balance to maintain. We do experience a sense of significance when we use our strength; this is natural. When we get the opportunity to use our talents, we have a special feeling of being on track with our destiny on this earth, and positive affirmations come our way. Because we naturally value our strength, we tend to feel significant when we use it; we feel like we are doing something of real importance.

But using our gifts can't provide ultimate meaning. Some people believe that if a door or two opened, allowing them to use their talents, a sense of significance would flow into their being. However, becoming all that we can be in life will never fulfill our hearts' longings for significance in an ultimate way.

Emotional wounding can bring on a crisis of significance. Many of us, at one time or another, have been wounded by authorities. Words like, "You will never amount to anything," or, "You are a failure" are seared into our emotions and leave us feeling like we have little significance. With this type of shaming, we might want to prove these authorities wrong by attaining a high level of success, status, wealth, or power. But when we set out on this course, there's an intense and constant pressure to perform. And we end up feeling less significant when we fail to meet the idol's impossible demands.

Many believe that merely looking inside themselves and unpacking their talents will satisfy their longing for significance. But ultimate meaning is not found in ourselves or our abilities; it comes from our relationship with Christ and having His heavenly perspective. We are "hidden with Christ," and our significance comes in Him.

Colossians 3:2-3: Set your mind on the things above, not on the things that are on earth. For you have died and your life is hidden with Christ in God.

Significance flows from our relationship with God. There is a process of this becoming a reality in our lives, whereby God weakens us so that we might become strong. It seems paradoxical that we become stronger after God makes us weak, but this is the divine pattern.

Look at Jacob. He was a wheeler-dealer, a mover-and-shaker, with a special knack for getting things done. In today's world, he would have been a great politician or businessman. His tenacity and ability to make things happen was his strength.

But then God overcame Jacob's strength. In a mysterious interaction, God wrestled with Jacob and touched him in his thigh.

Genesis 32:24-25: Then Jacob was left alone, and a man wrestled with him until daybreak. When he saw that he had not prevailed against him, he touched the socket of his *thigh; so, the socket of **Jacob's thigh was dislocated** while he wrestled with him. (emphasis added)*

After this encounter, Jacob was a different man. He was given a new name, indicating a new identity and nature.

Genesis 32:28: *He said, "**Your name shall no longer be Jacob, but Israel;** for you have striven with God and with men and have prevailed." (emphasis added)*

Jacob means "supplanter," while his new name, *Israel*, means "prince with God."[24] After his face-to-face encounter with God, Jacob's identity became attached to God; he was a prince *with* God. What a transformation!

Not only was Jacob's strength purified and empowered through his person-to-person-wrestling with God, but he became more secure. He was no longer dependent on his abilities to make things happen or to protect himself. God became his ultimate strength and his ultimate source of significance.

Many of us have faced the same situation, where we have to give up our strength, and the significance it gives us. Our strength dies, and with it, our old identity. And then, eventually, God resurrects it, but with a new identity in Christ.

Jacob's transformation came through a direct relationship with God. It wasn't something he could get by reading a book. His profound change came by meeting God first-hand.

It may be confrontative to meet the eternal God, the ultimate reality. We may stand in awe and say, as Jacob did, "I have seen God face to face, yet my life has been spared." (Gen. 32:30, NLT). But when we meet the One who is the ultimate source of meaning, our significance becomes ever-so-clear. After experiencing the infinite God, we see things differently and no longer look for meaning within our finite selves. And our significance is no longer in what we do in life but in Christ Himself. Significance idols fall away as our hearts become settled in Him.

Satisfaction Idols

We were made to be satisfied in God. We long to be fascinated, to find something that holds our attention, something full of awe and wonder. Fascination drew Moses to the burning bush, as he saw something curious and interesting in this "marvelous sight."

> **Acts 7:31:** *When Moses saw it,* **he marveled at the sight***; and as he approached to look more closely, there came the voice of the Lord. (emphasis added)*

And then, after Moses came with fascination to "look more closely," God satisfied his fascination with a revelation of Himself.

> **Acts 7:32:** *"I AM THE GOD OF YOUR FATHERS, THE GOD OF ABRAHAM AND ISAAC AND JACOB." Moses shook with fear and would not venture to look.*

Moses shook with fear as he was overcome with God's nature. But this encounter, which was so filled with awe, satisfied Moses' longing for fascination.

Our soul is designed to be captivated by the Person of God; His excellencies, character, and beauty. We are to *eat* (John 6:53), *drink* (John 4:14), and *taste* of His personality. He fills our being and satisfies us.

> **Psalm 34:8:** *O taste and see that the LORD is good; How blessed is the man who takes refuge in Him!*

IDOLS

We are meant to be fascinated by our Bridegroom and to be fulfilled as He reveals Himself. This kind of bridal intimacy, where our personality meets His, is the deepest and most satisfying to our soul. To know God and His glorious attributes is *life* to our soul (John 17:3).

We will seek something to captivate us. Maybe it's the arts, sports, or education. Perhaps, we are taken in by science and all it can decipher. In today's world, technology enthralls us and continually gives us some new gadget that holds our focus and enchants us.

Others get excited by people, with all their glamour and glitz. They are star-struck by political leaders, athletes, or actors. Just the thought of being in the presence of one of their heroes is enough to take their breath away and weaken their knees.

But God is the most fascinating person in the universe, and knowing His glory is the only thing that will satisfy our longing for awe. Most people can't fathom being spellbound by God's beauty and majesty. It is inconceivable that the unveiling of God's Person is exciting, or that there are treasures in His being that are more compelling than any earthly thing.

But this is why God has placed this longing for satisfaction in us; *He* fulfills this desire. Moses was fascinated by the burning bush, looked more closely, and met the God of glory.

Deep down our hearts yearn for the ultimate satisfaction, which comes by meeting the living God. He satisfies our hunger, and then our souls, driven by fascination, want more of Him.

Psalm 84:2: *My soul longed and even yearned for the courts of the LORD; My heart and my flesh sing for joy to the living God.*

Many Christians know, at least theologically, that God is almighty, eternal, majestic, and utterly different from anything created. They can point to the Scriptures that describe His attributes. Yet, to personally meet such a God and to be fascinated by Him may be a foreign concept.

We may get excited about things that surround God and doing things for Him. But doing for Him and focusing on God's activity in the Outer Court can keep us from developing an intimate relationship with Him in the Holy of Holies.

There is also a difference between sensing God's presence in the Holy Place and experiencing God's Person in the Holy of Holies. Just because we sense God's presence doesn't mean we have a heart attachment to Him or are experiencing the attributes of His personality. God's great invitation for all of us is to come into the Holy of Holies, where we experience the wonders of His nature.

Mike Bickle, the leader of the International House of Prayer in Kansas City, has seen his share of disillusioned ministers seeking God's hand and not His face. Bickle speaks about one such minister in his book, *The Pleasures of Loving God*:

...I was doing a large conference in Europe with a well-known man of God, and I was witnessing powerful demonstrations of the Holy Spirit. After the meeting, I could hardly wait to ask him what he felt when, during the service, a lady screamed out in joy after being instantly healed. I was very surprised by his answer.

He said, "I was glad for her, but personally I have grown accustomed to such demonstrations." Then he continued, "I still feel the same way in a lonely hotel room after the meeting: bored." He went on to describe his bitterness from various disappointments that had a hold of him.

I remember thinking, "Surely doing miracles in Jesus' name would cause life to be filled with excitement." I blurted out those words and he responded, "At first that's how we all feel. But over time we are confronted with our own spiritual bankruptcy if we don't encounter God in a deep and continued way."[25]

Many have not genuinely experienced the riches of God's nature. So, they don't realize God actually delivers the goods; He is more exciting, fascinating, and captivating than anything else. Once a person experiences God's nature, they know He is the main show in town: "the fountain of life."

Psalm 36:9: *For with You is the fountain of life; In Your light we see light. (emphasis added)*

As A.W. Tozer points out, a lack of hunger for God indicates that someone has not actually been *meeting* God.

Sure, they preach about Jesus dying for us and say, "Now if you believe that and accept Him everything will be all right." But there is no fascination, no admiration, no adoration, no love, no fear, no wonder, no yearning, no awe, no longing, no hunger, no thirst. I wonder if they have really met God at all. How could they and not be elevated into a holy atmosphere of adoration?[26]

The process of *fascination, seeking, and being satisfied* in Jesus can be seen in the story of Queen of Sheba meeting King Solomon.

1 Kings 10:2-7: *Arriving at Jerusalem with a very great caravan—with camels carrying spices, large quantities of gold, and precious stones—***she came to Solomon*** and* *talked with him about all that she had on her mind. Solomon answered all her questions; nothing was too hard for the king to explain to her.* **When the queen of Sheba saw all the wisdom of Solomon and the palace he had built...she was overwhelmed.** *She said to the king, "The report I heard in my own country about your achievements and your wisdom is true. But I did not believe these things until* **saw with my own eyes.** *(NIV - emphasis added)*

The Queen of Sheba had such hunger to be in Solomon's presence, to meet with him in person, that she traveled a great distance. She had to see him with her own eyes; it had to be first-hand. As Solomon unveiled truth and explained things to her, she experienced something that was heavenly and beyond herself. She was overwhelmed with the wonder and glory surrounding him.

Similarly, we are to be fascinated and satisfied in Jesus. He refers to Himself as the "something greater" than Solomon.

Matthew 12:42: The Queen of the South will rise up with this generation at the judgment and will condemn it, because she came from the ends of the earth to hear the wisdom of Solomon; and behold, something greater than Solomon is here.

Sadly, some have given up on being fascinated by God. Yet there remains a burning within to meet the One who is both mysteriously attractive and completely satisfying.

The souls of men naturally seek something which will bring rest and peace of mind, something that will satisfy and delight them

~*John Owen* 27

Family Idols

The family is foundational for both the individual and society in general. Because much good comes from the family, there is a tendency to turn it into an idol. Many look to it to meet their needs for safety, security, sanctification, significance, or satisfaction.

We met one gentleman who had recently lost his elderly father. We marveled as he told us about his father's wonderful attributes and how supportive he was throughout his entire life. Here was a model father, something you rarely see.

But now that his father was gone, he didn't know what to do. His world seemed to be collapsing in on him, as the man who had been a pillar through every situation and every crisis, was no longer there. Although his father had a profoundly positive influence on his life, he had become overly dependent on him. His father had become his god, as it were. With his father's passing, he had lost his source of security.

Thankfully, as we prayed with him, the Holy Spirit gave him a beautiful revelation of how God wanted to be a father to him. It was a sacred moment when he, with tears rolling down his face, cried out to his Heavenly Father to replace his natural father.

Most of the time, with family idolatry, several members are linked together. For instance, family members may all bow down to the idol of *family unity*. So, the idol requires parents, siblings, or even extended family, to above all else, give their allegiance to one another. The family idol promises certain "payoffs." This is why it's so alluring. But it also requires strict adherence to codes of conduct. "Do whatever it takes to maintain family cohesion, and everything will be ok," the idol says.

Of course, if one of the members stops functioning in their role, it creates quite a stir. Tensions rise when one cog in the wheel decides to shift their trust away from the family and onto God. One thing's for sure; when the family idol is threatened, there will be a strong reaction.

For those who want to make a change, and give up on the idol, setting healthy boundaries can be especially difficult. To change the family dynamics seems like a violation of something sacred. We often get a deer-in-the-headlights look when we suggest setting up boundaries with relatives. "Can I really do that?" people ask with bewilderment. We then say, "Wouldn't you do that if your friend behaved that way?" "Well, yes, of course, but this is my *family*!" is their response.

Some have a lifetime of dysfunctional, even destructive relationships with family members. Yet they struggle to make a change, believing boundaries will cut off their only source of security.

Others see it is as part of their Christian duty to love "unconditionally," which they interpret as giving themselves as a kind of sacrificial offering to the family. So, they can't imagine putting down a boundary as it seems so ungodly to them. Although this love-without-boundaries has an appearance of godliness, it's not healthy. In reality, turning a blind eye to dysfunctional behaviors is more about bowing down to the family idol and its requirements than about loving family members.

When Jesus walked the earth, he would not allow His natural family to become an idol. Not only did He keep God first in His heart, but he identified more with His spiritual family. He radically redefined the concept of family.

Mark 3:31-35: Then His mother and His brothers arrived, and, standing outside, they sent word to Him and called Him. A crowd was sitting around Him, and they said to Him, "Behold, Your mother and Your brothers are outside looking for You." Answering them, He said, "Who are My mother and My brothers?" Looking about at those who were sitting around Him, He said, "Behold My mother and My brothers!" **For whoever does the will of God, he is My brother and sister and mother.***" (emphasis added)*

Obviously, those who *do the will of God* may include natural family members, but this is not always the case. To assume so is to align with people who don't share the same values or motivations. God is not their Lord.

Even as a child, Jesus had his parents in their proper position. He submitted to His parent's authority and honored them but would not allow them to be in the exalted position of His Heavenly Father.

Luke 2:49-51: And He said to them, "Why is it that you were looking for Me? Did you not know that **I had to be in My Father's house?***" But they did not understand the statement which He had made to them. And He went down with them and came to Nazareth, and* **He continued in subjection to them***, and His mother treasured all these things in her heart. (emphasis added)*

Jesus warns us of a genuine temptation to love family members more than Him. He boldly states:

Luke 14:26: "If anyone comes to Me and does not hate his own father and mother and wife and children and brothers and sisters, yes, and even his own life, he cannot be My disciple."

Hate is a pretty strong word, but it underscores how the family, potentially one of the most wonderful things, can capture a heart and become an idol.

Parents have the responsibility of showing *God's* nature in a natural, tangible way so that their children can transfer this understanding, dependence, and affection onto the Lord. When children leave home, they are to "cleave" not only to their spouse but to God Himself.

Mark 10:7: *For this cause shall a man **leave his father and mother,** and **cleave to his wife** (KJV - emphasis added)*

Deuteronomy 13:4: *Ye shall walk after the LORD your God, and fear him, and keep his commandments, and obey his voice, and ye shall serve him, and **cleave unto him**. (KJV - emphasis added)*

Generational Idols

Parents pass good and bad things to the succeeding generations and, unfortunately, this includes their idols. The idols that fathers and mothers have attached to influence children in both *natural* and *spiritual* ways.

Parents naturally teach and model their beliefs before their children. For instance, when a father believes the most important thing is money, the children see this ideology walked out before their natural eyes.

Or, if a mother believes that image is everything, she may emphasize the importance of physical appearance. The children hear with their natural ears the importance of dressing and looking the part and are taught it is the key to getting opportunities or acceptance.

HERE ARE SOME COMMON GENERATIONAL IDOLS:

Hard work gives me value
Material possessions give me significance
Money gives me influence and safety
Love is all that matters
Compassion is all that matters
Giving to others makes me valuable
I will never have enough resources, so I have to hoard things
Doing practical things is most important
Poverty equals godliness
Independence makes me significant
Education makes me valuable
Being part of a group makes me safe
Having everything in order makes me secure
A keen intellect gives me value
Planning brings security
A strong leader is an answer for everything
An authority figure will keep me safe
Community is the answer to everything
Withdrawing from people keeps me safe
Self-expression gives me significance
Standing out as an individual is prideful, so I will withdraw
Conformity with a group gives me significance and security
I have to push down emotions to be acceptable and godly
Religious works sanctify me

Unity gives me security and must be maintained at all cost
Individualism gives me significance
I have value if my family accepts me
My family has to "bless" what I am doing in life
I am significant because my family is "upper class"
Prominence in the community gives me significance
I am valuable because I am successful
I am significant because I am a "blue-collar worker"
Blaming people keeps me from feeling worthless
Abusing people gives me a feeling of significance
Finding a "scapegoat" makes me feel secure
Government is the answer to all problems
Avoiding government is the answer to all problems
My family will always be persecuted, so I will isolate myself
To avoid disappointment, I will not hope or dream
The occult is the way I get spiritual direction
The Masons are a source of protection, a brotherhood
Manipulation will get me what I want
Disaster is around the corner, so I won't take any risks
God won't help me, so I have to do everything for myself
I have to control people to keep them from abandoning me
I have to appease people to maintain safety
I have to bribe people to make things happen in life
I will distance myself emotionally to control people
Women are valuable if they are pretty
To feel secure, women should avoid certain roles
Real men are cold and don't show emotions
Real men are domineering
I will abandon people before they abandon me
I am a victim and require everyone's sympathies
I am valuable because of my ethnicity/nationality
I have significance because of my family heritage

I can get what I want through violence, aggression, and rage
I can get what I want by self-denial and peace-making
My ethnic group will always be persecuted, so I will withdraw
Parental Inversion: I will require my child to parent me
Alcohol/drugs will keep me from feeling pain and shame
Sex gives me ultimate satisfaction
Pleasure gives me ultimate satisfaction
Sarcasm keeps me safe
Religious rituals sanctify me
I can create my own righteousness through works

So, there are natural ways parents influence their children toward one idol or another. But there are powerful *spiritual* influences at work, as well. God allows the demonic influence of the parent's idolatry to be "visited" on the children.

Exodus 20:5: *You shall not worship them [idols] or serve them; for I, the LORD your God, am a jealous God, visiting the iniquity of the fathers on the children, on the third and the fourth generations of those who hate Me. (emphasis, brackets added)*

What does this *visiting* look like? A demonic spirit comes through an open door by prior generations to tempt, entice, and pressure the children to attach to the same idol their parents trusted in. Earlier, we discussed a case in the book of Hosea, where a "spirit of harlotry," stemming from the *parent's* idolatry, pressured the daughters to "play the harlot."

Hosea 4:12-13: *My people consult their wooden idol, and their diviner's wand informs them; For **a spirit of harlotry has led them astray**, And **they [parents] have played the harlot**, departing from their God.*

203

They offer sacrifices on the ops of the mountains And burn incense on the hills, Under oak, poplar and tere binth, Because their shade is pleasant. **Therefore your daughters play the harlot** *And your brides commit adultery. (emphasis, brackets added)*

Behind every idol is a demonic spirit exerting its influence. When someone attaches to an idol, they effectively open a "spiritual gateway," a legal entry, for a particular spirit to trouble the succeeding generations.

These spirits come with an offer: *Trust in their ideology, and your heart needs will be met.* Generational idols and every other type of god, vie for our allegiance. They are offering food for our soul-hunger, but there is "poison" in what they are providing.

Deuteronomy 29:18: *Make sure there is no man or woman, clan or tribe among you today whose heart turns away from the LORD our God to go and* **worship the gods of those nations***; make sure there is no* **root among you that produces such bitter poison.** *(NIV - emphasis added)*

Once we take a bite, this poison permeates our souls, and things start breaking down. The first thing to go is our mental comprehension. A mindset develops, which makes us obsess about what we must do and what life has to look like for us to feel secure.

Fortunately, God has a way out. He can purge our soul of the toxins we have taken in. The process of soul-restoration starts with us turning our backs on idols; this is where freedom begins. But, as we will see in the next section, getting free and staying free are two different things.

Replacing Idols with God

Getting rid of an idol, when it has taken root in our heart, involves *turning away*. We make a decision of the heart to remove our allegiance and dependency on a false god.

But *replacing* the idol is just as critical. Otherwise, one idol will be swapped out for another. It is said that *nature abhors a vacuum*. Well, this is also true of the human heart. It will not remain empty; something will fill the void. This is why the Apostle Paul not only emphasizes turning from idols but a "turning *to* the living God."

> **1 Thessalonians 1:9:** *For they themselves report about us what kind of a reception we had with you, and how you* **turned _to_ God _from_ idols** *to serve a living and true God. (emphasis added)*

Timothy Keller, in his excellent book *Counterfeit Gods,* gets to the heart of the matter:

> *Idolatry is not just a failure to obey God, it is a setting of the whole heart on something besides God. This cannot be remedied only by repenting that you have an idol or using willpower to try to live differently. Turning from idols is not less than those two things, but it is also far more. "Setting the mind and heart on things above" where "your life is hid with Christ in God" (Col. 3:1-3) means appreciating, rejoicing, and resting in what Jesus has done for you. It entails joyful worship, a sense of God's reality in prayer. Jesus must become more beautiful to your imagination, more attractive to your heart, than your idol. That is what will replace your counterfeit gods.*

If you uproot the idol and fail to plant the love of Christ in its place, the idol will grow back.[28]

Repenting from idolatry, without replacing the idol, brings us back to square one. Our hearts start looking for something else to attach to. Giving up an idol is only giving up on a bad source of nourishment. The soul continues to crave food and drink. The truth is our emotional faculty hungers and thirsts and then goes in search of food and drink. This soul craving motivates us and sets us on a course, just as the natural appetite does.

Proverbs *16:26: A worker's appetite works for him, for his hunger urges him on.*

If we eat and drink from the proper source, the *person of God*, our soul is satisfied, and it has the nutrients it needs for development and strength. If we partake of some idol, our soul is weakened and becomes addicted to bad food and drink. So, it's imperative that we not only turn *from* the bad source but *to* the good source (God).

Is it essential to make decisions by using our reason? Of course. But it is a deception to think that our life is only charted by mental judgments, and our behavior is the result of pure logic. No, we are motivated from the bottom-up, from the heart. If we don't face up to the fact we are designed with certain soul-hungers, we'll be mystified by the things we do. We'll be going along merrily, thinking we have all our ducks in line, and then we'll fall for something. An idol will draw us in. "How did this happen?" we ask ourselves. Well, our soul became parched, and we went in search of a drink in the wrong place.

Many believe the Christian life is about reading the Bible and doing what it says. They don't realize their heart has particular appetites, and these cravings of the soul are just as real as physical ones. And to deny this hunger makes them more vulnerable to eating bad fruit from the wrong tree. Some believe, as did Adam and Eve did, that if they can just get a hold of a set of facts, some wisdom, they won't need God. They think it is not necessary to be in a functional, dependent relationship with God; they can eat of the Tree of Knowledge, and all will be well. Because they don't recognize their need for the Tree of Life, they end up attached to an idol or moving from one idol to another.

Because idolatry often involves good things. It's difficult to see that we are indeed attached to an idol. And after we rid ourselves of one god, there's a tendency to turn another good thing into an idol. For instance, a person may *serve* to fulfill their heart-need for sanctification. They then realize they've become self-righteous, and serving has become an idol. So, they turn their backs on this idol. They find it's a great relief to no longer bow to the idol's demands to serve everyone all the time. But they don't understand that sanctification is a work of the Holy Spirit (Titus 3:5). And because they haven't internalized the truth that *God* sanctifies through Christ, they go after another sanctification idol. Does this search lead them to dark places, doing evil things? No, not necessarily. Usually, they go after another good thing. Maybe they turn prayer into their new sanctification idol. They have simply traded out one god for another to deal with the same heart-need for sanctification.

I knew a pastor who struggled with feelings of insignificance and would see-saw between two idols. He would try one significance idol: *lead people to feel significant.* And then when that failed, he switched to another idol: *get significance by being behind the scenes.* After leading in a church for a time, he would become restless when he wasn't given enough recognition. His leadership idol demanded more and more attention until finally, after becoming disillusioned, he would resign his duties. So, then he went in the other direction and onto his other idol, which required him *avoiding* leadership. In doing this, he took on false humility, expecting others to recognize him for being the "humble servant," the person who didn't need any title or limelight. Neither idol met his need, yet back and forth he went. Had he replaced the idols with God, his heart would have settled into a healthy sense of significance.

Whether we are defending shame or trying to fill a heart need, idols always come up short and end up enslaving us.

Case Study: "The World-Changing Leader"

Bob has a natural gift of leadership. In his early years, he was the one rounding up the neighborhood kids and structuring the activities and games.

Bob's classmates tended to follow his lead. His teachers noticed he had such influence on his classmates that whatever he did, everyone seemed to fall in line. He pretty much set the tone for the class.

Bob is a born leader; he intellectually comprehends what's necessary to get from point A to point B and intuitively senses what's needed to steer a group to success. Along with these abilities comes an emotional value for leadership. Bob comes by it honestly. Many of his forefathers were military leaders, several having gone to West Point Academy. His father, an army officer, runs the house like military barracks, where everything is in tip-top shape, and orders are to be strictly followed.

Because Bob is keenly aware of good leadership, he respects his father's abilities and effectiveness. And, in many ways, his father is his hero. But Bob also feels something is missing. His father has very little personal time for him or his siblings, and his leadership is cold and detached. The situation is particularly vulnerable for Bob because he is a natural leader and values effective leadership. He admires his father's efficiency, but it hurts him when his father brushes him aside and doesn't take time to guide him in a hands-on way. The lack of personal attention during his childhood leaves him with an emotional deficit. Bob inherits the leadership abilities of his forefathers, but also their emotional coldness and distance.

Satan begins to take advantage of Bob's emotional vulnerability. A dark voice tells him, "Bob, there is something deeply wrong with you; that's why your dad doesn't spend time with you."Bob makes a decision that he will fight off these feelings of shame by successfully leading a large group of people. As so many do, Bob falls back on his strength. To counter the message of shame, he vows to become a world-class leader. This vow produces a mindset that pushes Bob to succeed at any cost. Failure is not an option because his success as a leader is a direct measurement of his value.

Bob works his way to the top of a global firm, but he is a controlling boss. He pushes those under his supervision to meet up to unreasonable standards of production and requires they spend endless hours in the office. Not only is Bob exhausted, but his employees, after being pushed and prodded by him every day, also run out of steam.

Bob ends up losing his job. He moves on and struggles with the same pattern in several companies; he quickly climbs to the top when others see his unique leadership abilities. Then, slowly but surely, things crumble when subordinates begin to complain about his domineering tendencies and his harsh style. Before he knows it, he is on the street looking for another leadership position.

One day, after listening to an evangelist on the radio, Bob receives Jesus Christ and is born again. Overwhelmed with gratitude, he desires to serve God in everything he does. Bob makes every effort to be a faithful follower of Christ, yet he struggles to be the kind of servant leader that he reads about in the Bible. The same old problems still surface at work, and he continues to be overbearing and abrasive.

Then the Holy Spirit begins a transformational work in Bob. He speaks persistently into Bob's spirit, "You need to lay down the success you are trying to achieve through leading." His first instinct is to push back against this voice of conviction. Bob's mind has been conformed to this way of thinking for so long that it's challenging to step into this unfamiliar territory.

Finally, Bob has had enough. He realizes, much like an alcoholic who knows they need help to stop drinking, that he needs God's help to overcome his "leadership addiction."

As he studies the Scriptures, the Holy Spirit highlights the Heavenly Father's nature. Rather than being distant, God has his "eye upon" Bob and is "directing his steps."

Psalm 32:8: I will instruct you and teach you in the way which you should go; I will counsel you with My eye upon you.

Proverbs 3:6: In all thy ways acknowledge him, and he shall direct thy paths. (KJV)

The concept that God is actively involved in his life is entirely foreign. But over time, as God imparts this truth into his emotions, doubts about his value fall away. Bob breaks out of a pattern that has been passed down from generation to generation.

As God restores Bob's inner man and renews his mind, his leadership takes on a different look. He no longer feels the intense pressure to validate himself as a leader and finds that he can think more clearly. There's an ease to his new leadership style, and he's able to analyze information and think outside of the box calmly.

Because his heart is attached to God, Bob is now able to lead out of a sense of security and no longer feels compelled to prove that he is an influential leader to satisfy his family's generational idol.

CHAPTER EIGHT

GOD'S PROCESSES OF RENEWAL

Comprehensive Heart Change

God heals our souls. What an amazing concept! We are not left in our brokenness but can look to God for a supernatural restoration, for our souls to be healed, restored, and renewed.

> *Isaiah 61:1: The Spirit of the Lord GOD is upon me, because the LORD has anointed me to bring good news to the afflicted;* **He has sent me to bind up the brokenhearted,** *to proclaim liberty to captives and freedom to prisoners (emphasis added)*

There are different ways that God heals us emotionally, and each has varying degrees of involvement on our part.

One way God heals emotions is by His divine touch. When the Scriptures talk about God "binding up the brokenhearted," it has the idea of God bandaging a wound.[29] The Divine Physician steps in to heal an emotional wound supernaturally, sometimes instantaneously

While this is one of God's methods of healing, restoration primarily comes as a byproduct of our relationship with Him. We participate in the process and have a personal exchange with God. Renewal transpires through communion with God; it doesn't just happen to us. We are renewed through epignósis knowledge of God.

Colossians 3:10: *...and have put on the new self who is* **being renewed to a true knowledge [epignósis-experiential, participatory knowledge]** *according to the image of the One who created him (emphasis, brackets added)*

As we increasingly become one with God, His transformative nature and attributes are imparted into our souls. Through unity with God our emotions and mind are restored and renewed.

John 17:23: *...I in them and You in Me, that they may* **be perfected in unity,** *so that the world may know that You sent Me, and loved them, even as You have loved Me. (emphasis added)*

All of us, at some point, have been wounded emotionally by interactions with imperfect people. What's God's answer? An interaction with Him, the perfect person. Our emotions, which were damaged and distorted, are healed by encountering God's person.

Healing of the soul is just one part of a comprehensive renewal that comes by experiencing God. Nature change, character change, sanctification, restoration of the emotions, and renewal of the mind are all part of the renovation of the soul that comes through intimacy with God.

Let's take another look at the bottom-up-approach to restoration and renewal.

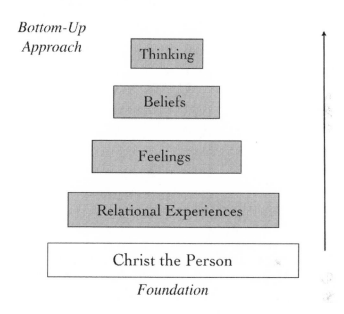

Bottom-Up Approach

Thinking

Beliefs

Feelings

Relational Experiences

Christ the Person

Foundation

Experiencing Christ gives us a divine deposit of emotional knowledge. Jesus becomes the foundation of our souls.When we have epignósis knowledge of Jesus, He is the internal reference point for all things. We see life, God, and ourselves differently.

After we've experienced Christ and felt His love, we have something for our beliefs to stand on. As Christ the Person is formed in us (Gal. 4:19), He is a foundation (1 Cor. 3:11) within our soul from which our beliefs can be changed, rightly aligned, and built upon.

The process works its way into our thinking. We go from relational *experiences* to changed *feelings*, to changed *beliefs*, to changed *thoughts*. After our mind is renewed, we no longer have a mindset distorting our thought processes, so we have the right mental perspective of God and ourselves.

As you can see, a renewed mind is the end result of experiencing God.

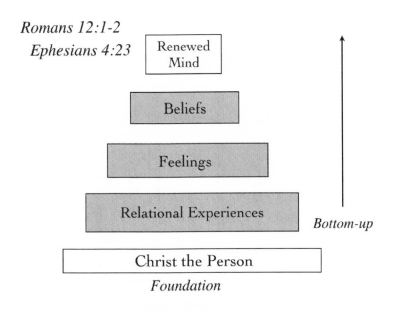

Paul tells us to "be" renewed or transformed (Eph. 4:23; Rom. 12:2).

Ephesians 4:23: *...and that you __be renewed__ in the spirit of your mind...(emphasis added)*

216

Romans 12:2: *Do not conform to the pattern of this world, but* **be transformed** *by the renewing of your mind. Then you will be able to test and approve what God's will is—his good, pleasing and perfect will. (NIV - emphasis added)*

Interestingly, to "be" is a *passive* word in Greek. So, renewal is not so much something we do, but it is yielding to God's Spirit and submitting to His processes of restoration.

Transformation and renewal start in the heart. The New International Version translation says that we should be made new in the "attitude" of our minds.

Ephesians 4:23: *...to be made new in the* **attitude** *of your minds... (NIV - emphasis added)*

Synonyms for "attitude" are sentiment or feeling. This indicates an emotional or heart attitude.[30] So, a change in the *attitude of the emotions* leads to a renewing of the mind. The Phillips translation captures this heart-to-head progression:

Romans 12:2: *...but let God* **remold your minds from within,** *so that you may prove in practice that the Plan of God for you is good, meets all His demands and moves towards the goal of true maturity. (Phillips - emphasis added)*

Although we are passive, we also *participate* in that we are in a connected relationship with the Holy Spirit. Loving God is actually part of being renewed. Because renewal flows from a relationship, when we choose to love God, we are attaching to Him and participating in our restoration.

We can't heal our emotions; at best, we can manage them. To a large extent, we are limited in what we can do to change our thoughts. Only God can restore emotions and renew minds.

For some, this is an entirely different approach to emotional and mental health. It has us dependent on God, requiring us to be attached to Him in a loving relationship. And it starts in the emotions rather than the mind.

If becoming more intimately acquainted with God is the focus of inner healing, then removing barriers to this transformative relationship becomes paramount. People often ask, "How do I get emotionally healed?" But better questions might be: *Am I growing in experiential knowledge of God? Am I attaching to God or an idol?*

1 John 5:21: *Little children, guard yourselves from idols.*

Reconciled with God

Up to this point, we have discussed how a relationship with God is key to everything. He satisfies our heart longings and restores our souls.

But we have a problem. We cannot approach God in our sinful state; we can't come in contact with the Holy One who fulfills our desires and heals us. In fact, the Bible says we are "enemies" of God. It's only when we accept what Jesus did for us and turn to Him (Rom.10:9) that we are "reconciled" to God.

Romans 5:10: *For if while **we were <u>enemies</u> we were <u>reconciled</u> to God through the death of His Son**, much more, having been reconciled, we shall be saved by His life. (emphasis added)*

218

Once we receive Jesus as our savior, we may draw near to God. At this point, we become a member of His family, a "child of God."

*John 1:12a: **But as many as received Him,** to them He gave the right to become **children of God**... (emphasis added)*

We go from being an adversary, wearing sin-stained garments; to a family member, clothed with robes of salvation and righteousness (Isa. 61:10). What a change!

Relationship with God, with all its life-giving benefits, begins after receiving Jesus. We are "rooted" in Christ Jesus *and then* are "built up in Him."

*Colossians 2:7: ...**having been firmly rooted** and **now being built up in Him** and established in your faith, just as you were instructed, and overflowing with gratitude. (emphasis added)*

Born from Above

The process of renewing our inner man starts with being "born again."

*John 3:5-7: Jesus answered, "Truly, truly, I say to you, unless one is **born of** water and **the Spirit** he cannot enter into the kingdom of God. That which is born of the flesh is flesh, and that which is born of the Spirit is spirit. Do not be amazed that I said to you, 'You must be **born again.**'" (emphasis added)*

When we are *born again*, we receive a "new heart."

Ezekiel 36:26: *Moreover, I will give you a new heart and put a new spirit within you; and I will remove the heart of stone from your flesh and give you a heart of flesh.*

Before this point, we have a limited ability to comprehend God; our understanding is obscured spiritually, mentally, and emotionally. With the new birth comes a new heart, one that is softened so it can comprehend.

After being born again, the Spirit of God dwells within us and gives us knowledge we would otherwise not have.

1 Corinthians 2:12: *Now we have received, not the spirit of the world, but the Spirit who is from God, so that we* **may know the things freely given to us by God.** *(emphasis added)*

It's life-altering to be born again. With this experience comes the setting of our inner compass towards God and the beginning of a soul renovation.

To seek soul restoration *prior* to receiving Jesus as Lord is putting the cart before the horse. The restorative benefits come within a covenant relationship *after* we have said "yes" to Him in a marriage-like commitment.

Growing in knowledge of Him, after the marriage vows, is something ongoing and to be enjoyed forever. God's eternal plan is to find a willing Bride to be transformed through oneness with His Son.

But this transformative relationship with Jesus is not automatic; it comes to those who seek Him as Bridegroom. A person may be born again but not grow in an intimate knowledge of Him, so there's little internal transformation.

The tabernacle of Moses in the Old Testament (Ex. 25-30, 35-40) gives us a picture of the progression from reconciliation to intimacy. The priest would start in the outer court where he would receive cleansing. Being washed was a necessary step to moving closer to God. Then the priest would move into the Holy Place, a place of prayer and provision. Finally, He would go into the Holy of Holies, where God unveiled the glories of His person.

Christians sometimes remain in the outer court after becoming a child of God. They are reconciled to God, cleansed, and born again through faith in Jesus. They have mental understanding they are forgiven and bound for heaven. But after being washed and born from above, there is minimal contact with God. They intellectually know they have been reconciled and have access to God, but they don't interact with Him.

Others move into the Holy Place, where they perceive God and communicate with Him through their spiritual faculty. They are excited when He interacts with them and are conscious of His provision for them. Although they pray to God and actively serve Him, there is little intimacy.

And then there are some who go into *the Holy of Holies*, where they meet God most intimately. They have a bridal love, flowing from their emotional faculty, and have a passion for knowing the excellencies of His nature. Their delight is in beholding God's character and beauty, and because they see Him, they are transformed inwardly.

Jesus "tore the veil" that separated us from God's glory. May we all go into the Holy of Holies to meet God face-to-face.

Mark 15:38: *And the veil of the temple was torn in two from top to bottom.*

221

Becoming a Living Sacrifice

After being born again, we have the seed of Christ in us and have been changed at the core. But the seed of His nature needs to grow into full-fledged fruit. As our soul is transformed and renewed, Christ's nature expands within us, and we bear fruit (Gal. 5:9, 22).

This process requires giving ourselves to God. We don't just give our service to God, but we offer *ourselves* to the Bridegroom.

Romans 12:1: *Therefore, I urge you, brethren, by the mercies of God, to* **present your bodies a living and holy sacrifice,** *acceptable to God,* **which is your spiritual service of worship.** *(emphasis added)*

Transformation requires a willingness to be a "living sacrifice," giving our entire person – body, soul, and spirit – into the Lord's hands so He might change us into His image. When the Bride gives herself to the Bridegroom, it is a sacrificial act of worship.

This is not a one-time act, but a continuous, *living* sacrifice. It requires an ongoing trust in God's sovereignty, allowing Him to use all circumstances in our lives to renew and mature our souls.

Some Christians are willing to receive instructions from God so that they might serve Him but are unwilling to give themselves so that He can transform them. The servant listens to instructions and makes sacrifices for God. But the Bride of Christ does much more; she gladly gives herself as a living sacrifice.

Being a living sacrifice requires us giving up control as well as a persevering trust when the feelings and insecurities of the past boil to the surface. God is in the midst of it all, taking apart our faulty foundations. This is a road less traveled. Many people get off the altar when the heat is turned up, and they find themselves thrust into a process where they are no longer in control. Their emotions scream, "Stop! Get off this altar and take back the reins of your life."

There is a mighty battle going on for the precious soil of the soul. God wants this territory, so the fruit of Christ's nature might grow. Satan's strategy is to sow weeds of self-protection and idolatry into this ground. This prevents the character of Jesus from being worked into the believer, which limits the expression of Christ to the world.

If there is a willingness, God will work powerfully in a person's life. I am amazed at how a simple prayer of surrender will open up the flood gates for God's renovation process. Suddenly, His invisible hand is orchestrating circumstances, bringing back memories and surfacing pain. God uses everything – all spheres of life – to expose the fault lines and then fills in the cracks with His nature.

Following ministry sessions, we often tell people, "God is going to start working the minute you walk out the door." Nevertheless, they are surprised to see just how comprehensive and intensive God's process is.

This highlights the importance of the *will*. Renewal comes by voluntary submission to God and allowing the Holy Spirit to do His work (Titus 3:5).

Often, after we identify a mindset and how it operates, people respond happily, "You are exactly right; that's what's going on in me." The diagnosis is received with great joy and a sense of relief. But sometimes there's an unwillingness to take the prescribed medicine; they don't want to be a living sacrifice and allow God to guide them through a process.

So, they choose to stay attached to their mindset, rather than redirecting their trust onto God. It feels safer to stay in the old, familiar pattern instead of cleaving to the Lord for security and accepting His terms. Even though they know it's baseless, they hope that if their spouse meets their needs, or if they get a better job, or are blessed with a new house, all will be well.

Others, after they realize they have a mindset, try to take the renewal process into their own hands. *They* determine just what's necessary for their healing and what God needs to do for them to be whole. However, instead of ridding themselves of their mindset, they end up reinforcing it.

For example, someone might come to find out they have a *control* mindset and want it removed. But their mindset tells them to take control of the renewal process. In a strange twist, their control mindset is telling them what they need to do to get rid of their control mindset. So, they may feel compelled to pray exactly right, or get in contact with the right people, or monitor all their thoughts and feelings. In doing this, they are yielding to their mindset, not to God. As a result, their control mindset remains firmly entrenched in their thinking.

God's processes of restoration and renewal are multi-faceted, to say the least. And they can either be *overt* or *covert*. An overt process requires more awareness of God and is an interactive and conscious experience. It involves engaging the Holy Spirit as emotions and thoughts come to the surface. This was true of Jean's process.

Or the renewal process may be *covert*, with God busy behind the scenes. It is more of an unconscious experience where the person is unaware of what God is doing. This was part of my process; I only had a vague sense of the Lord's under-cover workings. When it was over, I was different, but I couldn't put my finger on precisely what happened to me.

I believe this covert method was necessary for me because of my tendency to perform for God. It was essential for me *not* to know all the details so I wouldn't try to perform in my healing process.

This would have been counterproductive because He was trying to remove my performance mindset. So, God hid Himself and what He was doing. My challenge was in trusting Him and not leaving the altar He had chosen for me.

Jean, with her overt process, was more aware of what was going on. Because she is so connected to her emotions, it was second nature to be engaged with God and to express herself to Him. But the process went to another level as God uncovered pain and shame, traumatic incidents of the past, and tormenting mindsets.

The process was one of *feeling* and then *healing* of emotions. The Holy Spirit would resurface the shame in her emotions and then restore her soul. Once she was healed, and her shame removed, her mindset would give way because there was no longer a wound to protect.

Many days Jean lay in bed while she went through a kind of emotional surgery by the Divine Surgeon. It required trust in God and His care; she had to "be still and know that He is God."

> *Psalm 46:10: He says, '**Be still, and know that I am God;** I will be exalted among the nations, I will be exalted in the earth.' (NIV - emphasis added)*

There were times, because of the intensity of the experience, it was difficult for Jean to stay on the altar. But in this place of vulnerability, she met a God who is deeply concerned for her wellbeing and is full of lovingkindness.

> *Psalm 36:7: How precious is Your lovingkindness, O God! And the children of men take refuge in the shadow of Your wings. (NASB)*

In His wisdom and mercy, God will disrupt and dismantle mindsets. He does this by orchestrating circumstances so that we cannot do what our mindset requires. It may seem odd, but in a moment, He will set the dials of our life so that our mindset fails.

Initially, it can feel like things are taking a turn for the worst. Mindsets demand adherence, and when it's not possible to comply with their demands, they press with higher intensity. It's like restricting the flow of water on a hose, which forces the pump to work even harder.

God's disruptive work often comes on the heels of us relinquishing control to Him. He respects our wills, so if we choose to stay off the altar, He has a hands-off approach. But once we give Him the wheel, and present ourselves a living sacrifice, He starts driving the process. He begins dismantling the mindset.

When we are willing to let God run the show, He leads us with "His eye upon us."

> **Psalm 32:8:** *I will instruct you and teach you in the way which you should go; I will counsel you with **My eye upon you**. (emphasis added)*

It can be unnerving when God takes apart a mindset because it seems like our only source of security is being taken from us. It feels like the foundation we are standing on is giving way. And it is!

Because it requires us to be vulnerable and is not an overnight process, it may be tempting to get off the altar. But it is worth it in the end. We experience real freedom and peace as there is no longer a mindset tormenting us or obstructing our view of the Lord.

There is no more significant act of worship than giving ourselves as a living sacrifice. It is an act of betrothal to Christ

Jesus, "making ourselves ready for Him." What could be more glorifying to God?!

> **Revelation 19:7:** *Let us rejoice and be glad and* **give him glory***! For the wedding of the Lamb has come, and his* **bride has made herself ready***. (NIV - emphasis added)*

Wholeness and Holiness

There is a direct relationship between emotional health and personal holiness; *wholeness and holiness* go together. The healthier a person becomes in their soul, the more holy.

When I use the word *holy*, I am not just speaking of purity but being *set apart*. The Biblical understanding of holiness includes both. So, a holy person is pure but is also set apart unto God, distinct, and transformed in the inner man.

Emotional wounding produces self-protective mindsets. And mindsets tend to keep us from being transformed and renewed, so we are less holy and less God-like.

Some mindsets require ungodly behavior, like *control* or *manipulation*. But even mindsets with a noble goal, *like achieving success*, eventually result in sinful behavior. There are causalities along the way when a success mindset pushes someone to get to the top of the mountain, no matter who they step on during the ascent.

Now, you might argue that someone who has a mindset like *giving*, couldn't possibly act sinfully. But mindsets are all about self-protection, not Godly character. If a mindset is in play, benevolence isn't motivating the giver. Much like an alcoholic uses drink to medicate, they medicate their pain and shame by providing gifts or money. The minute they are unable to deliver, their mindset turns up the heat. Eventually, the pot boils over, and there's bad behavior.

After being born again, the Christian has at their core a change in nature (2 Cor. 5:17) and a propensity towards holiness (1 John 3:9). But there is still internal ground in the soul that must be taken before behaviors change. Part of this change is emotional healing; becoming whole as a person so we can be holy.

Thinking and behavior flow from who we are. If we aren't renewed in our emotions, behavioral change is an uphill battle. When God heals us emotionally, it ultimately influences our behaviors. So, He equips us for doing good by working in us.

Hebrews 13:21: ...equip you in every good thing to do His will, working in us that which is pleasing in His sight, through Jesus Christ, to whom be the glory forever and ever. Amen. (emphasis added)

Emotional healing and renewal of the mind allow the nature of Christ to grow in us. When His nature expands in our soul, holiness and godly behavior will follow.

God does a transformative work *within* us to make us more godly *outwardly*. As author Erwin Lutzer points out, godliness is something God works into our unconscious nature:

Unconscious godliness has the fragrance of God, whereas self-conscious godliness has the stench of hypocrisy. True godliness cannot be manufactured; it is something we must allow God to do for us. Unconscious godliness reflects the work of God in the soul.[31]

When we attach to God, His nature works its way into our unconscious being. This is how we become holy and distinct and how our behaviors change. More than anything, sinful behavior comes from a heart attachment to idols:

> **Colossians 3:5:** *Therefore, consider the members of your earthly body as dead to* **immorality, impurity, passion, evil desire,** *and* **greed, which amounts to idolatry**. *(emphasis added)*

> **Ephesians 5:5:** *For this you know with certainty,* **that no immoral or impure person or covetous man, who is an idolater,** *has an inheritance in the kingdom of Christ and God. (emphasis added)*

Rather than focusing on the symptoms, our behaviors, we would do well to redirect our hearts to the Lord. Part of this shift is allowing God into the vulnerable parts of the heart, rather than giving in to self-protection. If we cleave to a self-protective idol, we will remain unchanged and prone to sin.

Many remain in sinful patterns, simply because they have such low expectations when it comes to all that God offers. So, they continue to drink from the same, contaminated well.

As C.S. Lewis says, we are too easily satisfied with what the world has to offer:

> *We are half-hearted creatures, fooling about with drink and sex and ambition when infinite joy is offered us, like an ignorant child who wants to go on making mud pies in a slum because he cannot imagine what is meant by the offer of a holiday at the sea. We are far too easily pleased.*[32]

If we aren't satisfied with God and enjoying the treasures of His person, we will look for another source. Theologian John Piper sums it up nicely:

Sin is what you do when your heart is not satisfied with God. No one sins out of duty. We sin because it holds out some promise of happiness. That promise enslaves us until we believe that God is more to be desired than life itself (Psalm 63:3). Which means that the power of sin's promise is broken by the power of God's.[33]

May we make communion with the Holy One our primary goal in life so we too can become holy.

Repentance

The concept of repentance has been somewhat lost in the Church. Many understand repenting and turning to Christ for salvation, but not repentance as a way of life. Repentance unto salvation is a one-time event that *puts us in* heaven, but ongoing repentance *prepares us for* heaven.

Repentance is a vital, continuous process of turning our heart over to the Lord. Much like the children of Israel conquered the physical land of Canaan, the territories of our soul need to be taken over through repentance, piece-by-piece.

Some people view repentance as merely a change in behavior. They see the Christian life as following the moral teachings of the Bible and applying its wisdom to their lives. So, when they fall short, they see repentance as getting back to doing the right things.

However, it is much more. Repentance is not just saying "sorry" and then trying to behave appropriately. The essence of repentance is turning away from idols (1 Thess. 1:9) and toward God. It's a change in affection and attachment, a sacred, holy redirect of our heart to the Lord. And it's a continual process.

Repentance primarily has to do with the heart. Sinful behavior enslaves (John 8:34), and we need to turn away from it. But our heart attachments will ultimately hold us captive. Anything good or bad that we attach to from the heart will capture and control us.

We can be enslaved at a heart-level to a good thing like success. A success idol will run our lives. It will dictate who we hang out with, where we spend our money, how we allocate our time, how we plan our future, and what we need to achieve each day. If success is our idol, more of it is the last thing we need.

Our greatest fear should not be of failure but of succeeding at things in life that don't really matter

~D.L. Moody

When we disconnect from an idol and become attached to God, He meets our deepest needs, including our need for healing and holiness. Turning to Him makes us whole and holy.

Author John Eldredge ties repentance to holiness and healing:

"For the people's heart has become calloused; they hardly hear with their ears, and they have closed their eyes. Otherwise they might see with their eyes, hear with their ears, understand with their hearts and turn, and I would heal them." (Matthew 13:15)

Heal them. Jesus yearned for his people to turn back to him so that he could heal them. The "otherwise" means that if they weren't so hardheaded, they would turn to him and he would heal them. This truth is essential to your view of the gospel. It will shape your convictions about nearly everything else. God wants to restore us. Our part is to "turn," to repent as best we can. But we also need his healing. As Ephesians 1:4 says, God chose us to make us whole and holy through love. God will make known to us the path of life if we follow him. And as we do, we find along the path our need for wholeness and holiness.[34]

Repentance sounds pretty unattractive if it's just a matter of *not* doing things. But when it means shifting of our focus onto a beautiful Person, who brings "fullness of joy," it becomes attractive indeed.

__Psalm 16:11:__ You will make known to me the path of life; In Your presence is fullness of joy; In Your right hand there are pleasures forever.

What could be more wonderful than turning to a God who is full of delights? If we turn to Him, we get to experience His truth, His security, His love, and His beauty. Who wouldn't want to embrace this kind of repentance? Yet, we often resist it and hang onto our protective idols.

Breaking Inner Vows

An inner vow is a powerful mechanism within the human soul. Look at the Nazis, for example. After making an oath of allegiance to Adolf Hitler, they exhibited fanatical behavior; senseless and terrible things were done for their leader.

How could this happen? It was a clear case of the heart leading the head. The vow was a choice of the heart, which then distorted their thinking. This choice made from the volitional part of their being locked them into a twisted view of reality. After vowing to die for Hitler and his dark causes, they would throw themselves into the line of fire, even when the war was lost. This insane behavior became routine for them, blind obedience flowing from a vow they made in the past.

While this is an extreme example, it nevertheless highlights how this soul mechanism causes us to lose touch with reality and act irrationally. Once the vow is made in the heart, a mindset forms in our thinking.

Typically, it is emotional trauma which compels us to make inner vows. When we are wounded and feeling shame, we are vulnerable to ungodly ways of protecting ourselves.

The life of former President Richard Nixon illustrates how an inner vow works and how perilous its effects can be. When Nixon was a young man, he experienced shame and made a vow that he would *never be hurt again emotionally*. I believe a mindset developed in his thinking: *I will attack people so they can't hurt me.*

What were the effects of this vow? One minute, Nixon was clear thinking, and the next, when his mindset was operating, he was completely irrational and paranoid. It got to the point that just about everyone was an "enemy." He viewed his life through a narrow prism because of the vow made in his past. Nixon was a virtual prisoner of his own mindset. It had him questioning peoples' motives and pressed him to take action against those who were a perceived threat.

There was a way out of this inner crisis. Had Nixon turned to the Lord, he could have been transformed. But letting go of his vow would have been as formidable as facing a world dictator. He would have to give up on his protective idol and trust God to remove his shame.

The will is key. Inner vows start and end with our volition; we choose to make a vow, and we choose to break the vow. If we decide to keep our vow, God lets us have our way. Amazingly, He honors our will.

How do we break an inner vow? Verbally renouncing it is a powerful act. The Bible says what flows *forth from the mouth* reflects what's *in the heart* (Matt.15:18). So, a verbal renunciation is a way we can break a vow of the heart. When we renounce a vow, it's like breaking the flow of current in a closed circuit. The vow loses its power.

But there is another step, where God rewires our internal circuitry. This requires us to open the doors of our inner man to the Holy Spirit so He can do His work.

It's vulnerable to give ourselves in this way so that He can reshape and mold us, but God is merciful in the process.

Romans 12:1: *Therefore, I urge you, brethren,* **by the mercies of God,** *to present your bodies a living and holy* *sacrifice, acceptable to God, which is your spiritual service of worship. (emphasis added)*

Progressive Restoration & Renewal

One of the biggest misconceptions is that soul transformation is instantaneous. More often than not, it's progressive and depends on a living relationship with God. Scripture points to the progressive nature of renewal and transformation.

> **2 Corinthians 4:16:** *Therefore, we do not lose heart, but though our outer man is decaying, yet our inner man is* **being renewed day by day.** *(emphasis added)*

> **Colossians 3:10:** *...and have put on the new self who is* **being renewed** *to a true knowledge according to the image of the One who created him. (emphasis added)*

> **2 Corinthians 3:18:** *But we all, with unveiled face, beholding as in a mirror the glory of the Lord, are* **being transformed** *into the same image from* **glory to glory,** *just as from the Lord, the Spirit. (emphasis added)*

God is gracious in using a gradual approach to renewal because a person's identity is deeply tied to their mindset. They have depended on it for security, and it has, in many ways, shaped their view of the world. Instantly tearing down their internal house can be disorienting, to say the least.

The principle of progressive change can be seen when God tells the Israelites He would clear out nations "little by little."

*Deuteronomy 7:22: The LORD your God will clear away these nations before you **little by little**; you will not be able to put an end to them quickly, for the **wild beasts would grow too numerous for you**. (emphasis added)*

God changes us one a step at a time. It prevents demonic spirits from taking advantage of us when we are most vulnerable, just as the *wild beasts* would do to Israel. In a similar verse, God says the nations were to be driven out progressively until Israel had "increased."

*Exodus 23:30: **Little by little** I will drive them out before you, until **you have increased** enough to take possession of the land. (NIV - emphasis added)*

Christ must progressively increase in the soul of the believer. It's how territories of the heart are taken over and held and how demonic spirits are cleared out and kept out.

Our Heart is Like a Field

Once the seed of Christ is planted in the believer, God wants His character and excellencies to expand. His nature is to take over the field (1 Cor. 3:9) of our heart.

Mindsets are a kind of weed in the soil, which hinders the growth of the seed of Christ. They create barriers to relationship with God and limit the transforming work of the Holy Spirit.

What we attach to determines how much of the nature of Christ will expand in our soul. If we cling to mindsets, we will remain unfruitful, but if we cleave to Jesus (John 15:5), His nature will grow in us and we will bear fruit.

This increase of Christ's nature is what the Apostle Paul means when he speaks of Christ being "formed in" believers.

> **Galatians 4:19:** *My children, with whom I am again in labor until* **Christ is formed <u>in</u> you...** *(emphasis added)*
> Paul also says that Jesus was "revealed *in* him."

> **Galatians 1:15-16:** *But when God, who had set me apart even from my mother's womb and called me through His grace, was pleased to* **reveal His Son <u>in</u> me** *so that I might preach Him among the Gentiles, I did not immediately consult with flesh and blood (emphasis added)*

Some of us have had good heart ground, but then the soil becomes hardened and resistant. Although it has been plowed before, it is now dormant, or "fallow ground."

The nature of Christ does not grow in this kind of ground, but "thorns" do. Mindsets flourish in fallow ground. God wants us to "break up the fallow ground" of our hearts by opening ourselves up to Him.

This also involves making Him the primary object of our affections. In this way, we "circumcise" our hearts.

> **Jeremiah 4:3-4:** *For thus says the LORD to the men of Judah and to Jerusalem,* **"Break up your fallow ground***, and do not sow among thorns.* **Circumcise yourselves to the LORD** *and remove the foreskins of your heart, men of Judah and inhabitants of Jerusalem, or else My wrath will go forth like fire and burn with none to*

quench it, because of the evil of your deeds." (emphasis added)

Starving a Mindset

Many people live their entire lives with a mindset keeping their pain and shame at a low-grade-level. They may not be aware of it, but their mindset is at work below the surface.

And then God starts going after the mindset by *starving it*, not giving it what it craves. At this point, people become painfully aware there is a parasite in their soul.

God's disruption is designed to get to the core issue. He aims to uncover the emotional problem the mindset has been protecting. So, God starves the mindset by not giving it any food.

How does He do this? Sometimes it is as simple as not allowing things to work. For instance, a person with an *order* mindset is no longer able to keep everything in order. Again, God does this not to harm us but to free us. By putting pressure on the mindset and not allowing it to work, emotional pain comes to the surface. And this is precisely what the Lord is after. He is trying to get to the root issue, *the shame in the emotions*, that is fueling the mindset.

This process can feel like taking steps backward. Such was the case with one 23-year-old woman we met. A high achiever, she was as driven and successful as anyone I have ever known. After paying her way through college and getting straight "A"s, she had started her own business. She was full of confidence and even dressed the part. Yet something was amiss inside, and she knew it. I asked her if she would pray a simple prayer: *God, I give you permission to change and heal me.*

Two weeks later, she contacted us and was utterly distraught. "Nothing is working," she sobbed. God had simply not allowed her to perform. He was starving her performance mindset, not giving it anything to feed on. It exposed the reason she had become so dependent on performance in the first place: *shame from her childhood*. At first, it appeared that things were getting worse. But God was at work behind the scenes, doing a beautiful thing in this young lady. She came to understand a profound truth: her value was *intrinsic*, not based on her performances.

And through the process, she learned to feed on God, rather than the idol of performance. God desires to heal us, but He also wants us to transfer dependence away from our mindsets and onto Himself.

Starving a mindset is something the Lord regularly does with His children. It often catches them off guard because it can be an intense experience. But we shouldn't be surprised by "fiery" tests like this.

1 Peter 4:12: Beloved, **do not be surprised at the fiery ordeal among you,** *which comes upon you for your testing, as though some strange thing were happening to you. (emphasis added)*

Sometimes the Christian goes through seasons where it appears that all favor has been lost. Amid the testing, they feel like God, for some inexplicable reason, is not allowing them to fulfill their calling. "Why won't God allow me to use my gifts?" they ask despairingly.

But, trials are proof that we are God's children. And God is more concerned about developing our inner life and conforming us into His image (Rom. 8:29) than He is about activating our gifts. God wants to establish Jesus as our inner foundation (1 Cor. 3:11), even if it involves deconstructing our self-made houses. The process of starving and dismantling a mindset is Fatherly "discipline," a sign we are legitimate children of God.

> **Hebrews 12:7-8:** *It is for discipline that you endure; God deals with you as with sons; for what son is there whom his father does not discipline? But if you are without discipline, of which all have become partakers, then you are illegitimate children and not sons.*

Father God knows what's best and doesn't want us to endure the long-term heartache, frustration, and stress associated with mindsets. Thus, it's vitally important to let the Holy Spirit do His work of extracting mindsets from our soul. How He does this work is His prerogative.

> **Titus 3:5:** *He saved us, not on the basis of deeds which we have done in righteousness, but according to His mercy, by the washing of* **regeneration and renewing by the Holy Spirit** *(emphasis added)*

Also, mindsets are idols. And idols demand, distort, disappoint, and are dissatisfying. So, detaching from them and attaching to the Lord allows us to experience Him and to have Him meet our heart needs. Going through the process of starving a mindset is worth it as God gives Himself as a replacement, and we have lasting security.

But what about those who take things into their own hands, unwilling to submit to God's processes? What about *illegitimate children*? Scripture indicates that God gives them over to their "self-made" idol.

> **Isaiah 50:11:** *Behold, all you [enemies of your own selves] who attempt to kindle your own fires [and work*

*out your own plans of salvation], who surround and gird yourselves with momentary sparks, darts, and firebrands that you set aflame!—**walk by the light of your self-made fire and of the sparks that you have kindled [for yourself,** if you will]! But this shall you have from My hand: you shall lie down in grief and in torment (Amplified Bible - emphasis added)*

Milk and Meat

Up to this point, we have discussed how a living relationship with God is key to everything. It is the way we are restored and transformed into Christ's image, and it is life for our souls. Without this connection, we don't experience life in God.

Some Christians realize that relating to God is of utmost importance but struggle to meet Him face-to-face. Feelings of shame are so pervasive that the thought of sitting at the Lord's feet and communing with Him is very unsettling. In fact, it's downright scary.

They need "milk," which is easily digested. Milk concepts are things like: we are unconditionally loved, God delights in us, and we have intrinsic value. As well as truths such as: Jesus paid for our sins (Col. 2:14) and justified us (Rom. 3:24), we are saved by His grace (Eph. 2:8), He gives us His righteousness (Phil. 3:9), and He died for us when we were sinners (Rom. 5:8).

These are primarily things that God has done and is doing *for us.* Milk is reassuring and helps us to meet the person of the Lord, so we can grow and mature.

*1 Peter 2:2: ...like newborn babies, long for the pure **milk** of the word, so that by it you may **grow** in respect to salvation (emphasis added)*

Many have transferred an image of their earthly father, who was angry and abusive, onto God. So, they are terrified to sit in God's presence, and the last thing they want to do is to open themselves up with the most vulnerable places of their heart. For these folks, receiving and digesting milk helps them stay engaged with God. Even the mature Christian, at times, needs to go back to drinking milk, especially if they feel like pulling away from God.

So, what is "meat"? It's both *complex* issues that are difficult to comprehend as well as *weighty* topics. It includes things like: accountability before God (1 Pet. 4:17), walking in righteousness (Titus 2:12), carrying the cross (Luke 14:27), God's judgment (Rom. 2:16), self-sacrifice (Matt 20:27-28), consequences of behavior (Matt.16.27), and the fear of the Lord (Ps.19.9).

The meat is more difficult to digest and requires maturity and discernment. In a nutshell, it involves issues related to *our responsibility* as an adult believer.

Just as a child grows naturally and takes on more responsibility, so it is with the Christian in relationship to God. Babies are not expected to understand things or to have responsibilities. They aren't held accountable for anything; they just drink milk provided for them by their parents. But as they grow and can stand on their own two feet, they eventually have to digest meat. And as Christians, there are meaty issues we face: our days on earth will be assessed by God and have eternal consequences. What we do with our lives really does matter to God.

*2 **Corinthians** 5:10: For we must all appear before the judgment seat of Christ, so that each one may be*

242

recompensed for his deeds in the body, according to what he has done, whether good or bad.

It's breathtaking to think that what we attach to in this life will bear on our relationship to God for eternity. Christians building things that will be burned up at the end of this life is indeed a meaty concept.

1 Corinthians 3:15: If any man's work is burned up, he will suffer loss; but he himself will be saved, yet so as through fire.

That being said, this kind of meat is hard to digest if there's not a clear understanding that we are loved, accepted, valued, and cleansed. If we never digest this milk, the mere mention of God's correction or the fear of the Lord causes us to pull away in shame. We choke on the meat and feel unloved, insignificant, or even unsaved.

It takes maturity to grasp *all* aspects of God's nature. God is a tender Father, but He is also a judge. The accepting love of God and the fear of the Lord fit properly together:

1 Peter 1:17: If you address as Father the One who impartially judges according to each one's work, conduct yourselves in fear during the time of your stay on earth.

When people understand they are loved and accepted, they are much more open to receiving correction (meat). It never ceases to amaze me how willing people are to look at themselves, confess their sins, and turn to the Lord if they're confident they will not be shamed or abandoned in the process. We can turn to God without fear of being shamed. Even if we have done evil, we need not fear Him. For the sake of His name, the Lord will not abandon us.

Samuel says it plainly:

*1 Samuel 12:20-22: Samuel said to the people, "**Do not fear. You have committed all this evil, <u>yet do not turn aside</u> from following the LORD**, but serve the LORD with all your heart. You must not turn aside, for then you would go after futile things which cannot profit or deliver, because they are futile. **For the LORD will not abandon His people on account of His great name**, because **the LORD has been pleased to make you a people for Himself**" (emphasis added)*

If we are in a covenant relationship with God, He will discipline us but never forsake us: He will not violate His covenant.

*Psalm 89:32-33: Then I will **punish their transgression** with the rod and their iniquity with stripes. But I will **not break off My lovingkindness** from him, nor deal falsely in My faithfulness. **My covenant I will not violate**, nor will I alter the utterance of My lips. (emphasis added)*

Holding onto both meat and milk requires maturity, a maturity of discernment. It means digesting meat without feeling abandoned by God. Training one's senses to understand the "word of righteousness," while at the same time holding onto the "elementary principles."

*Hebrews 5:12-14: For though by this time you ought to be teachers, you have need again for someone to teach you the **elementary principles** of the oracles of God, and **you have come to need milk and not solid food**. For everyone who partakes only of milk is not accustomed to* *the **word of righteousness**, for he is an infant. But solid food is for the mature, who because of practice **have their senses trained to discern good and evil**. (emphasis added)*

Drinking in the milk of the elementary principles sets the stage to take on more meaty concepts. The mature can digest meat because they have come to know God's voice and character. They've gone beyond the "basic teachings" of Christianity into a greater "understanding" of God.

Hebrews 6:1-3: *So, let us stop going over the **basic teachings about Christ** again and again. **Let us go on instead and become mature in our understanding**. Surely, we don't need to start again with the fundamental importance of repenting from evil deeds and placing our faith in God. You don't need further instruction about baptisms, the laying on of hands, the resurrection of the dead, and eternal judgment. And so, God willing, **we will move forward to further understanding**. (NLT - emphasis added)*

Sometimes people stay immature because they choose to feed off of an idol. This was the case with the church of Corinth. The apostle Paul was only able to give them milk because of their immaturity, which showed up in their competitiveness and over-identification with certain "apostles."

1 Corinthians 3:1-5: *And I, brethren, could not speak to you as to spiritual men, but as to men of flesh, as to **infants in Christ**. **I gave you milk to drink, not solid food**, for you were not yet able to receive it. Indeed, even now you are not yet able, for you are still fleshly. For* *since there is jealousy and strife among you, are you not fleshly, and are you not walking like mere men? **For when one says, "I am of Paul," and another, "I am of Apollos,"** are you not mere men? What then is Apollos? And what is Paul? Servants through whom you believed, even as the Lord gave opportunity to each one. (emphasis added)*

They turned their leaders into idols, which stunted their growth. In order to mature, they needed to let go of this leadership idolatry and attach to the Lord.

The Bride of Christ – One with God

Transformation and restoration are the outworking of something more central and magnificent. Oneness with God is the supreme goal, the chief reason He has brought us into existence. From Genesis to Revelation, the Bible speaks of a covenantal relationship with God and His people. God is the Husband and the Bridegroom.

In the Scriptures, the oneness between a husband and wife is compared to Christ and the Church.

***Ephesians 5:31-32:** As the Scriptures say, "A man leaves his father and mother and is joined to his wife, and the two are united into one." This is a great mystery, but it is an illustration of the way **Christ and the church are one.** (NLT - emphasis added)*

246

Biblical transformation is relational. Restoration of the soul and renewal of the mind depends upon meeting the Lord in a bridal way. God calls us to a sacred relationship where He unveils the richness of His person through a marriage-type union.

The Lord desires to reveal Himself and impart His nature into the soul of the believer through oneness. Not only does the Bride take on His likeness through oneness, but her soul is renewed and restored as she experiences the God who is beautiful, secure, righteous, faithful, powerful, wise, kind, consistent, patient, fatherly, just, fascinating, and holy.

Puritan writer John Owen said:

> *So, in carrying on this union, Christ freely gives himself to the soul. Precious and excellent as Christ is, he becomes ours. He makes himself available to us with all his graces. So, the spouse says, "My beloved is mine. In all that he is, Christ is mine. Because he is righteousness, he is the Lord my righteousness. Because he is the wisdom and power of God, he is made to me wisdom" (Jer. 23:6; 1 Cor. 1:30).[35]*

God beckons us to *cling* to Him so that we might become one with Him.

> **Deuteronomy 10:20:** *You shall fear the LORD your God; you shall serve Him and **cling** to Him, and you shall swear by His name. (emphasis added)*

What does it mean to *cling* to God? The same word is used in Genesis when speaking of a husband and wife cleaving to one another.

247

Genesis 2:24: Therefore shall a man leave his father and his mother, and shall **cleave unto his wife***, and they shall be* **one** *flesh. (KJV - emphasis added)*

This kind of heart-to-heart attachment changes us. Bad relational experiences with imperfect people are replaced with experiences with the perfect One. He restores us by giving His nature, which has no "variation or shifting shadow."

James 1:17: Every good thing given and every perfect gift is from above, coming down from the Father of lights, with whom there is no variation or shifting shadow.

The need for a relationship with God is universal. We can't properly comprehend truth or be transformed without the relational exchange that comes through oneness with Him.

The Bridal Responsibility

Becoming one with God is critical; it is the way our soul receives life. So then, what is the Bride's responsibility?

A covenant relationship with God is a two-way street. In E.W. Kenyon's book, *The Blood Covenant*, we see the depths of what it means to give ourselves in such a relationship:

In Genesis 15:6, God made a promise to Abraham, and it says that, "Abraham believed God and it was reckoned to him for righteousness."

This word "believe" here in the Hebrew means not only a "loving trust," but it also means "give yourself wholly up," or, "to be a part of Himself," or "go right into Him," or "the unqualified committal."[36]

Giving ourselves *wholly up* is our part of the covenant. This goes back to being a living sacrifice (Rom. 12:1), in that we give the entirety of our person to God. The Bride is to give herself and to open her heart to the Lord.

We are the doorkeepers of our hearts, and we choose to open ourselves up to experience and reciprocate love. In Revelation, Jesus tells the Church of Laodicea that He will fellowship with those who "open the door" to Him.

> **Revelation 3:20:** *Behold, I stand at the door and knock; if anyone hears My voice and* **opens the door, I will come in to him** *and will dine with him, and he with Me. (emphasis added)*

Jesus will come in if we open ourselves. It is our responsibility to open the doors of our emotional faculty so that He can come in, and so we might direct our love out. It takes two persons to "dine" with one another, to have fellowship with one another. Both are seeking to know and love the other, and both have opened themselves to one another.

In the heart of the Bride is the desire to know her Bridegroom's nature. Beholding Him is the primary goal both now and in eternity. She appreciates the necessity of the outer court, but she desires to meet Him in the Holy of Holies.

From the Bride's view, blessings are secondary to experiencing Him. Knowing Him is the ends, not a means to an end. The Bride is after personal knowledge of God, knowledge "in the face" of Jesus Christ.

2 Corinthians 4:6: For God, who said, "Light shall shine out of darkness," is the One who has shone in our hearts to give the Light of the **knowledge of the glory of God in the face of Christ**. *(emphasis added)*

God is experienced most profoundly by those who want to know His person, who desire to behold His beautiful and awe-inspiring attributes.

Some expect God to pour out His treasures and excellencies even though they have little regard for His person. This is like Shishak, the king of Egypt, going into the temple of God and stealing all the treasures from the house of God.

2 Chronicles 12:9: So, Shishak king of Egypt came up against Jerusalem, and took the treasures of the house of the LORD and the treasures of the king's palace. He took everything; he even took the golden shields which Solomon had made.

He had no respect for the sacredness of God's house; he just took the treasures. Similarly, I think sometimes we seek God's riches and the things He can give us without respect for the sacredness of His person.

Those who only hunger for spiritual revelations, or are overly fascinated with the spirit world, won't see God as clearly. Their motivation is to partake of things, to *take God's treasures,* not to connect with His personality.

But God reveals the treasures of who He is with those who revere Him as Lord.

Psalm 25:14: The friendship of the LORD is for those who fear him, and he makes known to them his covenant. (ESV)

We wouldn't share our secrets, hopes, and deepest feelings with someone who didn't respect us, or who had little interest in us personally. But we would share ourselves with someone who wanted to know us for who we are as a person. We would reveal the treasures of our inner man with someone who valued us. This is also true of God.

Emil Brunner, a great 20th-century theologian, asserted that God's "self-communication" is to those who choose to love Him and reciprocate His love back:

God communicates himself in love: and this happens in the fullest sense only when his love is known in responding love. Unless this happening takes place, self-communication cannot consummate itself.[37]

God's *self-communication* is within the bonds of a marital-type covenant relationship. That is, God reveals Himself to those who love Him for who He is. The attitude and motivations for seeking God do make a difference as to how much of Him we will see.

Matthew 5:8: *Blessed are the **pure in heart**, for they shall **see God**. (emphasis added)*

Because God loved us first (1 John 4:19), there's a great responsibility for us to respond to His love.

Communication and Communion

Now let's go back to some earlier diagrams. The spiritual faculty allows us to hear God's voice and to perceive in the spiritual realm.

*Information from God or perceived
from spirit realm does not
necessarily lead to an emotional/
heart connection or transformation*

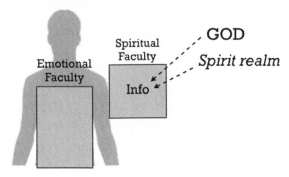

We may sense God and receive information from Him, but this spiritual perception does not necessarily equate to heart-to-heart intimacy with Him.

Spiritual sensitivity and connectivity are essential. In fact, we can't move on to communion with God without some level of connection between the Spirit of God and our spirits. But a revelation of spiritual information is different from a revelation of God's nature.

Moses didn't just receive information from God; he communed with Him. God says he would communicate with other prophets via "visions" and "dreams," but with Moses, it's different.

*Numbers 12:6-8: And the LORD said to them, "Now listen to what I say. If there were prophets among you, I, the LORD, would reveal myself in visions. I would speak to them in dreams. But not with my servant Moses. Of all my house, **he is the one I trust**. I speak to him **face to face**, clearly, and not in riddles! **He sees the LORD as he is**. So why were you not afraid to criticize my servant Moses?" (NLT - emphasis added)*

Notice the depth of intimacy between the Lord and Moses; it's *face-to-face*. And the Lord *trusts* Moses and reveals Himself within this covenantal relationship. Moses is allowed to see the person of the Lord.

Spiritual communication is just the first step to something more significant: *communion*. Communing with God includes the spiritual faculty because we connect with Him spirit-to-spirit. It is an experiential, ginóskó-type knowing.

But communion also requires the emotional faculty. We use the emotional faculty to connect with other persons, including God's person. There's a two-way flow as we love God and open ourselves to His love. In this way, we *participate* in knowing Him and receive epignósis knowledge. Epignósis is the most life-giving and transformative knowledge and comes through "beholding" God's person.

*John 6:40: For this is the will of My Father, that **everyone who <u>beholds</u> the Son and believes in Him <u>will have eternal life</u>**, and I Myself will raise him up on the last day (emphasis added)*

Beholding the Lord is more than a vision or mental picture of Him; it is a kind of inward "seeing," where God's nature is experienced.

> **2 Corinthians 3:18:** *But we all, with unveiled face,* **beholding** *as in a mirror* **the glory of the Lord,** *are being transformed into the same image from glory to glory, just as from the Lord, the Spirit. (emphasis added)*

Helps Word Study defines *glory* as God's "infinite, intrinsic worth."[38] So, you could say, beholding Him is experiencing His worth as a person.

Communion with God Person-to-person

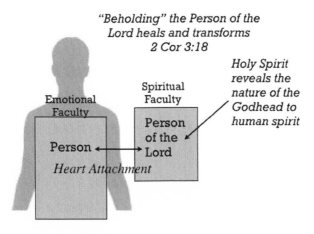

Various Bible characters came in contact with God's glory. They beheld the *infinite value* of His nature. And once they did, getting another view of Him became the supreme goal of their lives. God Himself became their destiny.

King David's one request of God was to see His "beauty" (Ps. 27:4). The Apostle Paul considered everything as "dung" compared to "the excellency of the knowledge of Christ Jesus my Lord" (Phil. 3:8, KJV). Moses wasn't satisfied with being led by God, but plead to see more of His nature, saying, "Show me Your Glory" (Ex.33:18). Everything came into perspective for Job when he saw the Eternal One: "My ears had heard of you but now my eyes have seen You" (Job 42:5, NIV).

God answered the longings of these men with more revelation of Himself. This is true today; God reveals Himself, the beautiful attributes of the Godhead, to those who *want* to see and experience Him.

Jesus said He would "disclose" Himself to those who love Him. So, to some extent, we experience God's love for us when we love Him.

*John 14:21: "He who has My commandments and keeps them is the one who loves Me; and **he who loves Me will be loved by My Father**, and **I will love him** and will **disclose Myself** to him." (emphasis added)*

Epignósis is the most precise and highest form of knowledge because it comes through communion with the One *who is the truth* (John 14:6). It has us participating in knowledge by loving God; Emil Brunner would say it's knowledge *consummated* in love.

255

Demystifying the Mystical

Even with clear scriptural examples of communing with God, some have argued that this deeper life is reserved for a select few. Or that those seeking union with God are a fringe group of "mystics," strange folks who operate outside the banks of normal Christianity.

To say that there is no Scriptural basis for an experiential relationship with God runs contrary to His Word. Experiencing God is a central message of the Bible. To encounter God and be satisfied in who He is, is most glorifying to Him.

John Piper says it like this: "God is most glorified in us when we are most satisfied in Him."39

All of us are to be mystics if defined as being in a loving and experiential relationship with God. The Christian life without this kind of interaction is disconnected from the "Vine" (John 15:4) and void of life.

Jesus speaks of "eating his flesh" and "abiding in Him," which is an experience of His person. This is how we have the fullness of life and bear the fruit of His nature.

> *John 6:53: So, Jesus said to them, "Truly, truly, I say to you, unless you **eat the flesh** of the Son of Man and drink His blood, you have **no life in yourselves**." (emphasis added)*

> *John 15:4: **Abide in Me**, and I in you. As the branch **cannot bear fruit** of itself unless it abides in the vine, so neither can you unless you abide in Me. (emphasis added)*

The Apostle Paul had a mystical quality. Not only did he enjoy experiencing God, but he wanted others to know God in the same intimate way.

Paul incorporated all his faculties into his walk with God. With his keen intellect, he understood complex spiritual concepts and was able to articulate doctrinal truths. His spiritual faculty was involved in personal communications with God and was used for building up others. And with his emotional faculty, he experienced the excellencies of God's person.

For Paul, having a mystical side was essential to the Christian life. It wasn't something spooky, but part of an everyday walk with God.

A.W. Tozer brings mysticism down to earth:

He (the mystic) differs from ordinary orthodox Christian only because he experiences his faith down in the depths of his sentient being, while the other does not. He exists in a world of spiritual reality. He is quietly, deeply, and sometimes almost ecstatically aware of the presence of God in his own nature and in the world around him. His religious experience is something elemental, as old as time and acquaintance with God by union with the eternal Son. It is to know that which passes knowledge."[40]

Case Study: "The Woman of Excellence"

Sally is a woman of excellence. As a Christian, she believes that God does things with excellence, and every activity should be done to reflect this part of His nature.

She gravitates towards 2 Peter 1:3: "seeing that His divine power has granted to us everything pertaining to life and godliness, through the true knowledge of Him who called us by His own glory and excellence."

When people do things half-heartedly, it gets under Sally's skin. She believes when you do something, you should do it well. It's not the quantity of the work, but the quality that matters. She'd rather do a few things well than be busy with lots of frivolous projects.

Even in the most mundane things of life, Sally's mind picks up on the little details that make things shine. And she senses intuitively how things fit together correctly and what's necessary to bring forth the gold.

Her parents have loved her unconditionally and encouraged her to spread her wings. Sally never doubts her parents' love. Yet, something is troubling her; as a young adult, she lives a reclusive life, unable to leave the safety of the nest.

Sally is emotionally paralyzed not because of any one particular issue, but because of what it means to have "problems." In her view, having any problem is proof that she is not a person of excellence. So, any issue, no matter how insignificant, is shaming. Her drive towards excellence torments her. Whenever she's in public, she reviews every situation, every relationship, every perceived failure. She cringes as she examines the long list of "issues" that she believes proves she's not making the grade.

As the message of shame escalates, she grabs onto a solution: she will hide. This will prevent any more failures, which always seem to point to her lack of excellence. Sally decides the best way to avoid the terrible feeling of shame is to stay clear of people and activities. And because Sally has trusted avoidance as a means to help herself, a mindset forms.

Sally becomes even more boxed in when a second mindset develops to help her in those rare cases where she's in public. This mindset has Sally searching for qualities that people like and then changing her personality. Like a chameleon, she modifies herself to her environment and continually changes her persona. But this leads to more frustration. Sally's mindsets torment her, there's constant pressure to change herself, and no relief from her shame.

At this point, there seem to be no options. Sally simply must be a person of excellence, yet her problems are evidence she is not. Finally, after years of struggle, she finds help from Christian counselors. When they ask her what her issues are, she sheepishly answers, as if revealing a dark sin, "My problems are so numerous...I don't know where to begin?"

After hearing her confessions, one of the counselors responds with, "Sounds fairly normal for a girl your age." Sally, for the first time in years, feels a glimmer of hope that perhaps her problems are not what they appear to be. Leaning forward in her chair, Sally asks, "Do you mean I am not more broken than other people?" "Well," says the counselor, "I am convinced your biggest problem is that you think you have a problem."

For months Sally gleefully repeats this phrase to herself: "My only problem is that I think I have a problem." Light has been shed on the false beliefs and mindsets. After clearly seeing the distorted thoughts that have been spinning around in her head, she takes a more objective view of things. Sally realizes that her drive towards excellence is a powerful force for good or bad. It is good if she directs it outward for the glory of God, but bad if used as a means to determine her value as a person.

This insight helps her make the first steps in her healing process. She understands how vulnerable she is to measuring her value based on excellence, so she begins to focus on her identity in Christ. The Holy Spirit also begins a transformation process in her emotions and mind so that she no longer feels the need to constantly self-assess.

One verse becomes very special to her on the journey to freedom:

Psalms 139:14: I will give thanks to You, for I am fearfully and wonderfully made; Wonderful are Your works, and my soul knows it very well.

"Lord," Sally prays, "I see in your Word that I was made fearfully and wonderfully, which means you made me a person of excellence. I ask that you would help my soul to know this truth.

CHAPTER NINE

PRACTICAL CONSIDERATIONS

God has outstretched arms and pursues us as a passionate Bridegroom. The cross is an example of how far He will go to be in relationship with us.

But we can also draw near to God and build a relationship with Him. There are things we can do to have face-to-face meetings with Him, where we can know God and be known by Him. There are ways to fix our gaze on the Lord and practical things that will help us grow closer to Him.

Setting Heart on God

Intimacy with God is our highest call and greatest joy. No one will regret embarking on the sacred journey to see "the Desire of All Nations" (Hag. 2:7, NKJV).

One might ask, "Where do I begin?" A first step is to set your heart on God, to make the Lord Himself the treasure of your life, what is most precious to you. So, knowing and attaching to Him becomes priority number one.

The first commandment tells us to love God, which means we set our affections on Him. We love God *with our heart.*

> **Matthew 22:37:** *Jesus replied: "Love the Lord your God* **with all your heart** *and with all your soul and with all your mind." (NIV - emphasis added)*

We have the capacity to direct our love; this is a function of our emotional faculty.

> *Then Samuel spoke to all the house of Israel, saying, "If you return to the LORD* **with all your heart**, *remove the foreign gods and the Ashtaroth from among you and* **direct your hearts** *to the LORD and serve Him alone; and He will deliver you from the hand of the Philistines." (emphasis added)*

Everyone has the awesome responsibility to make God the object of their love. It's sobering to think that we are given a choice to love Him and to enter into His courts (Ps. 100:4).

David could have had anything in this world, yet he chose to set his heart on God. In these verses, you can see his intentionality.

> **Psalm 16:8:** *I have* **set the LORD continually before me**; *Because He is at my right hand, I will not be shaken. (emphasis added)*

> **Psalm 18:1:** *And he said, I* **will love thee**, *O LORD, my strength. (KJV - emphasis added)*

> **Psalm 57:7:** *My heart is* **fixed**, *O God, my heart is fixed: I will sing and give praise. (KJV - emphasis added)*

But loving God is more than just raw determination and willpower; it takes God's grace for us to be able to love God. And we have to experience Him to be able to reciprocate His love.

We choose to love God by setting our affections on Him and beholding His beauty. But there is also a sense in which our love for God grows as we feel Him delighting, approving, attaching, and taking pleasure in us. You could say, we experience God experiencing us. Love is born out of and flourishes within an experience of oneness with God.

> *1 Corinthians 8:3: but if anyone loves God, he is known [ginóskó – experienced] by Him. (brackets added)*

Everything begins with God. He starts by appealing to us to seek His face.

> *Psalm 27:8: When You said, "Seek My face," my heart said to You, "Your face, O LORD, I shall seek."*

Setting our affections on God is necessary, but not the end of the story. There's seeking and seeing the Lord. Both are important. After David was near to God, there was no other place he'd rather be:

> *Psalm 84:10: For a day in Your courts is better than a thousand outside. I would rather stand at the threshold of the house of my God than dwell in the tents of wickedness.*

The Apostle Paul experienced great depths of relationship with God because he considered intimacy with Him to be worth any price, process, or suffering. God was the great "prize" Paul sought.

Philippians 3:12-14: *Not that I have already obtained it or have already become perfect, but I press on so that I may **lay hold** of that for which also **I was laid hold of by Christ Jesus.** Brethren, I do not regard myself as having laid hold of it yet; but one thing I do: forgetting what lies behind and reaching forward to what lies ahead, **I press on toward the goal for the prize** of the upward call of God in Christ Jesus. (emphasis added)*

This *laying hold* of God was hardly a passive, disinterested approach to knowing God. It has the idea of grabbing someone and pulling them down, like a football player tackling someone.[41] What a remarkable picture of passionately seeking after the most wonderful person in the universe.

But while Paul was intensely seeking God, he also understood that he was just responding to God's pursuit of him. Jesus had first laid hold of him, so Paul's passion was born out of God's love for him.

The loss is severe if we let the first commandment slide to second. Not only do we miss the wonderful communion with the Lord, but emotional wounds and mindsets remain in our souls. Damage in the soul obscures the very thing we are seeking: a *clear view of the Lord.*

Setting our hearts on God is a way we come close to Him so He might come close to us.

James 4:8a: *Draw near to God and He will draw near to you.*

Quieting

Habakkuk 2:20: "But the LORD is in His holy temple. Let all the earth be silent before Him."

Most people in today's world are busy going from one activity to another. And there are audio and visual messages inundating them every minute of the day. This creates a kind of noise in the soul, which makes it difficult to hear the Lord's voice or to interact with Him.

I know an elementary school teacher who has what she calls "carpet time" with her students. All activities stop during carpet time. There's no agenda; nobody is required to learn the ABCs, arithmetic, or history. And there are no physical requirements, other than being quiet (as much as possible for third graders) and listening to others.

Carpet time is for person-to-person interaction. The only goal is to know and be known. It's a time of sharing one's inner life, and then listening to others as they do the same. I think we need the same kind of thing with God, where we have carpet time and share ourselves with Him and He with us. This requires us quieting ourselves, our "flesh," before Him.

Zechariah 2:13: "Be silent, all flesh, before the LORD; for He is aroused from His holy habitation."

Someone I know had a conversation with Mother Teresa about her time with God. Mother Teresa said, "I spend four hours in the morning with God, and do you know what I do during that time? I don't do anything." She practiced the discipline of simply being still and quiet before the Lord. Stopping the noise in her soul and sitting with the Lord allowed her to commune with Him.

Finding a quiet physical environment is helpful. But even amidst busyness and activity, we can make it our practice to quiet ourselves and look at God inwardly. As A.W. Tozer points out, intentionally "gazing" on God can be done at any time and in any place.

Many have found the secret of which I speak and, without giving much thought to what was going on within them, constantly practice the habit of inwardly gazing on God. Even when they are compelled to withdraw their conscious attention in order to engage in earthly affairs, there is within them a secret communion going on. Let their attention be released but for a moment from necessary business, and it flies to God once again."[42]

Meditation

Meditation is a powerful way of relating to the Lord. By *meditation*, I mean contemplating the meaning of Scriptures, mentally mulling over the text.

The goal in meditation is not just to understand the propositional truth of Scripture, but to see and experience God.

All the faculties work together beautifully in meditation. The mind focuses on the meaning of the text, the Holy Spirit unveils the truth to the spiritual faculty, and finally, the emotional faculty is touched with the experience of God's person.

The goal in meditation is not to stretch the Scriptures beyond their clear grammatical meaning and context. But, instead, to think on the text, so the Holy Spirit might illuminate it and give us a more personal and experiential revelation of God.

266

Meditation can help us meet with the person of Christ, who the Scriptures are pointing to:

John 5:39-40: *"You search the Scriptures because you think that in them you have eternal life; it is these that testify about Me; and you are unwilling to come to Me so that you may have life."*

We do need a mental understanding of what the Bible says about the Lord, but we can go deeper with meditation; we can come into contact with the Lord Himself.

The Holy Spirit loves to reveal Christ to us through the Scriptures. Not just what He has done for us, but who He is. For instance, take this verse:

1 Peter 3:18: *For Christ also died for sins once for all, the just for the unjust, so that He might bring us to God, having been put to death in the flesh, but made alive in the spirit.*

The process of meditation is top-down; it starts with mental understanding. Mentally, we see what Christ did for us; we grasp the logical truth. But after meditating on the verse, *thinking about it*, the Holy Spirit illuminates the text so that it impacts the spiritual and emotional faculties. Christ's devotion, sacrificial love, and reconciliation are understood in a different way. Meditation turns a mental concept into a personal experience of Christ's character.

The Holy Spirit desires to reveal the wonders of the Godhead in this way. He is in the midst of our contemplations about the Lord. This doesn't mean He changes the grammatical meaning of Scripture, but He certainly brings it to life and enhances it.

Many know Jonathan Edwards as one of the greatest thinkers and theologians in American history. But few realize how he used his mind to develop a heart attachment to God. Edwards spent countless hours meditating on Scripture and God's creation. Desiring to see the beautiful attributes of God, he set his mind on the living Lord of the Bible.

Edwards saw a difference between knowing about God and experiencing Him.

Thus there is a difference between having an opinion, that God is holy and gracious, and having a sense of the loveliness and beauty of that holiness and grace.There is a difference between having a rational judgment that honey is sweet and having a sense of its sweetness.[43]

By continually meditating on and contemplating "divine things," Edwards loved God with his mind (Mark 12:30).

My mind was greatly fixed on divine things, almost perpetually in the contemplation of them. I spent most of time in thinking of divine things, year after year; often walking alone in the woods, and solitary places, for meditation, soliloquy, and prayer, and conversation with God...[44]

How did God respond to Edwards' passionate focus and meditations? The Holy Spirit made the person of Christ come alive in the Scriptures for Edwards.

Sometimes, only mentioning a single word caused my heart to burn within me; or only seeing the name of Christ, or the name of some attribute of God.[45]

Edwards also meditated on God during his walks in nature. As he looked at and pondered the wonders of creation, the Holy Spirit magnified God's beauty and excellence. Edwards couldn't seem to find enough adjectives to describe God's glorious attributes.

...I walked abroad alone, in a solitary place in my father's pasture, for contemplation. And as I was walking there, and looking up on the sky and clouds, there came into my mind so sweet a sense of the glorious majesty and grace of God that I know not how to express. I seemed to see them both in sweet conjunction; majesty and meekness joined together; it was a sweet, and gentle, and holy majesty, and also a majestic meekness; and awful sweetness; a high, and great, and holy gentleness...

...God's excellency, his wisdom, his purity and love, seemed to appear in everything; in the sun, moon, and stars; in the clouds and blue sky; in the grass, flowers, trees; in the water and all nature; which used to greatly fix my mind. I often used to sit and view the moon for a long time; and in the day, spent much time in viewing the clouds and sky, to behold the sweet glory of God in these things; in the mean time, singing forth, with a low voice my contemplations of the Creator and Redeemer.[46]

I think the meditative life of Jonathan Edwards is a model for every Christian who wants to draw near to God. It's an intentional way to love and experience Him.

Self-Awareness

True wisdom consists in two things: knowledge of God and knowledge of self

~John Calvin

Becoming aware of what is inside ourselves is necessary if we want to relate to God and others. Relating to God is much more than developing our spiritual senses to hear His voice better. We engage Him with our entire soul: our mind, sense of self, will, emotions, values, personality, and strengths.

We have to identify what's in our emotional faculty to share ourselves with God and people. This requires us becoming a kind of detective, curious to search out what lies deep down inside our hearts.

The Bible tells us to "watch over" our hearts.

Proverbs 4:24: *Watch over your heart with all diligence, for from it flow the springs of life.*

We can't very well watch over our hearts if we are unaware of our feelings. So, we need to become proficient at identifying what brings us joy and sadness and what angers, motivates, inspires, captivates, and makes us want to withdraw. These are all things that reside in our emotional faculty.

One of the most important things we can do is uncover damage in our emotions and discover what the wounding is about specifically. When we do this, we'll find there's a message of shame taunting and tormenting us. There will also be some false beliefs and a mindset telling us how to avoid that shame.

There can be profound discoveries when we look inside and become aware of what we feel, where our thoughts are coming from, what we believe, and what's motivating us.

Becoming self-aware is not an end in itself. We don't want to be consumed with what's going on inside us or become self-focused; this isn't healthy. But self-awareness is required if we're going to share ourselves with God and people.

Self-awareness may also be a part of an emotional healing process. If we allow the Holy Spirit to, He will help "search" our inner man. God can be in the midst of our self-searching if we intentionally open ourselves up to Him.

Proverbs 20:27: *The spirit of man is the lamp of the LORD, searching all the innermost parts of his being.*

Awareness played an integral role in Jean's renewal process. When her emotions were triggered, she realized it was a signpost directing her to something significant, something that needed to be understood and processed. She became adept at picking up on what was going on inside herself, whether it was pain and shame, a false belief, or a mindset.

For some, examining emotions is difficult because they are detached from this part of their being. Their emotional faculty is like an island on the other side of the world, which they've never searched out.

Others recognize the importance of this distant island but feel it's fraught with danger. It seems far too vulnerable to explore this uncharted territory of the heart.

But self-awareness is an essential part of opening ourselves up to experiencing love and connection. Relationships require we show ourselves, our true selves, which means we have first to explore our inner man and find out what lies within. Self-revelation only comes with self-awareness.

Journaling

Once we have become self-aware and have identified our emotions, we can then open the doors to our emotional faculty and reveal what's inside.

Journaling, writing down our feelings, is a way to express our emotions to God. In this way, we become more connected to Him. When journaling, we need to express all of our feelings: the good, bad, and ugly. Some might say this is a pointless exercise because God already knows what we feel. Or they see it as blasphemous to express negative feelings to a holy God.

But it's important to share our true selves, so we can experience the joy of being known and receiving God's unconditional love for us. As we write down what we feel and express everything to Him, even things we may be ashamed of, we begin to understand God's "perfect love."

> *1 John 4:18: There is no fear in love; but **perfect love casts out fear**, because fear involves punishment, and the one who fears is not perfected in love. (emphasis added)*

Sure, God is serious about conforming us to His image and wants us to have a pure heart and godly character. But He doesn't love us because we have a pure heart. Thank goodness for that!

God's perfect love casts out any fear we might have of being turned away by God. King David understood this. He was confident that he would not be rejected because of his sin or any darkness in his heart. Rather than turning away in shame, he met God face-to-face with all that was in his heart.

In the Psalms, we see David's personal journal to God. He takes everything to Him, expressing both his positive and negative feelings. Rather than keeping things inside, he opened himself up and trusted that God would change his heart and forgive his "hidden faults":

Psalm 51:10: Create in me a clean heart, O God, and renew a steadfast spirit within me. (emphasis added)

Psalm 19:12: Who can discern his errors? **Acquit me of hidden faults.** (emphasis added)

So, journaling is one way of expressing ourselves to God. As we put pen to paper and communicate from the deepest part of us, we feel known and loved, and become emotionally connected to God.

Processing with God

We may become aware of and express our emotions to God, but still not engage Him. In other words, we may, in a mechanical sense, say things, but not process our inner life with the Holy Spirit.

Jean found, in her journey, God was listening and attentive to her expressions. At first, she had to trust that He would be there when she shared herself and presented herself before Him. But over time, after processing with God, there was a growing expectation that He would have answers and would restore her. As she engaged the Holy Spirit and brought her feelings and thoughts to Him, she experienced His active involvement with her.

Sitting before the Lord and processing with Him became a way of life, and the Holy Spirit responded to Jean's intentionality. When she couldn't make heads or tails of her feelings or thoughts, she counted on the Holy Spirit's help to sift through and make sense of things. She brought the Holy Spirit into the process by asking Him, "Why am I feeling this way? What is my mind telling me? Why did I attach to a mindset?"

Jean also had to be willing to stay on the altar, as painful emotions and shame came to the surface. It was challenging to remain with the process when a mindset would press her and tell her that she needed to go back to familiar territory. She had to trust God's sovereign hand through what was, at times, a confusing and unsettling experience.

But God was in the middle of Jean's interactive process, restoring her emotions and freeing her from the torments of her mindsets. He was responding to her request to "search out her heart."

Psalm 139:23: *Search me, O God, and know my heart; Try me and know my anxious thoughts.*

Worshiping God

Worshiping God is praising Him for who He is. This may include musical instruments and singing songs (Ps. 33:3), but it is primarily an expression of emotions, where we exalt God's character and attributes. In essence, worship is a loving adoration that flows from our person to His.

Worship requires we use our spiritual faculty to connect and communicate with the Spirit of God. True worship is a spiritual endeavor.

274

John 4:23: *"But an hour is coming, and now is, when the* **true worshipers will worship the Father** **in spirit and truth**; *for such people the Father seeks to be His worshipers. (emphasis added)*

We also use our emotional faculty to express and lift God up in worship. This faculty allows us to have a back-and-forth where we experience an attribute of God and then we reciprocate, worshiping Him for that part of His nature.

God has revealed His nature through the Scriptures, and if we are born again, we have some understanding of who He is. Based on these revelations of His character, we have a starting point for our worship. And then when we choose, from our heart, to praise Him, there is often a further unveiling of His attributes.

Worship includes a thankful heart for what God has done for us, but in its highest form, it is praising God for who He is. It is "ascribing" to Him specific attributes that are part of His nature.

Psalm 96:7: *Ascribe to the LORD, O families of the peoples, ascribe to the LORD glory and strength.*

1 Chronicles 16:29: *Ascribe to the LORD the glory due His name; Bring an offering and come before Him; Worship the LORD in holy array.*

When exalting God's attributes as a person, we have a connection to the excellency of His character.

Sometimes we start the process by praising God for His goodness, holiness, or beauty. God may then show that particular attribute of His personality to us in a more significant way. So, if we exalt God's holiness, we get a greater understanding of His holiness. I think that the angels worshiping God "day and night," do so because they have seen God's holiness to some degree. But then, as they praise God and say, "holy, holy, holy," there is more revelation of His holiness.

> ***Revelation 4:8:*** *And the four living creatures, each one of them having six wings, are full of eyes around and within; and day and night they do not cease to say, "HOLY, HOLY, HOLY is THE LORD GOD, THE ALMIGHTY, WHO WAS AND WHO IS AND WHO IS TO COME."*

True worship is God-centered. I don't think much of today's Christian music, which focuses on God helping and elevating us, is very worshipful. And because it doesn't honor God's person, the worshiper doesn't get to experience Him.

I've been in corporate settings where there's a desire to magnify God, where people have worship-filled hearts that want to exalt Him. And in unison, they cast their gaze to Heaven and onto God. In these extraordinary times, when everyone humbly worships, God often looks down from His lofty position and reveals more of His nature.

I wonder if Isaiah was worshiping God as the supreme ruler of the universe for years before seeing God "on the throne, lofty and exalted."

> ***Isaiah 6:1:*** *In the year of King Uzziah's death I saw the Lord sitting on a throne, lofty and exalted, with the train of His robe filling the temple.*

Worship puts God in His rightful and high position, exalting His glorious attributes. The creature is in a low position and worshiping the Lord for all that He is. This is what it means to worship Him "as God."

> **Romans 1:21:** *Yes, they knew God, but they wouldn't* **worship him as God** *or even give him thanks. And they began to think up foolish ideas of what God was like. As a result, their minds became dark and confused. (NLT - emphasis added)*

When we worship Him as God, we are putting our trust in who He is and what He provides for us. If we worship Him as the protector, we come to know Him as the protector.

Or if we worship God for His beauty, we see and experience more of His beautiful character. Not only is our need for satisfaction met, but we become more fascinated in Him and long to see more of His nature.

By worshiping Him *as God*, we look to Him to meet our heart needs for safety, security, sanctification, significance, and satisfaction.

And there's another benefit which follows: instead of our mind becoming "dark and confused," it's filled with light and understanding.

God's Sovereignty

I have suggested several practical steps that may help in relating to and experiencing the Lord. Setting our hearts on God, quieting, meditation, expressing through journaling, processing with God, and worship are things we can do to engage God.

At the same time, God's sovereignty cannot be understated. Sometimes in focusing on what *we* do, we forget that God

Almighty acts according to *His* will, initiative, mighty power, and infinite wisdom. He is His own person.

If this is not clearly understood, we can put too much pressure on ourselves and get over-focused on our part of the relationship. We may question if we love God as we should, are seeking Him fervently, or are pure enough in our devotion. Even if this is the case and we need to grow in these areas, staring at ourselves doesn't help. In fact, if we become overly circumspect and self-focused, we may disqualify ourselves and not engage God anymore.

Better to trust in the excellency of God's character and good intentions in the relationship. He is motivated by a desire to relate with us and, in many ways, initiates and completes things.

> ***Philippians 1:6:*** *...being confident of this, that **he who began** a good work in you **will carry it on to completion** until the day of Christ Jesus. (NIV - emphasis added)*

God brought us into existence, provides salvation and sanctification, and even gives us a heart to love Him. Because He is the "beginning and the end," we need to focus on and attach to Him.

> ***Revelation 22:13:*** *"I am the Alpha and the Omega, the first and the last, the beginning and the end."*

When we are focused on ourselves, it's difficult to stay connected to God. A driving instructor will tell us that we tend to drive the car where we are looking. So, we need to focus our eyes down the highway, rather than one side of the road, or a few feet ahead. If we focus our inner eyes on God, we will move toward Him.

It's also important to remember that God is active in our lives. Without this perspective, we tend to take things into our own hands. Abram and Sarai felt the need to help God fulfill His promise by producing a son through Hagar, Sarai's maid. But then God Almighty stepped in and said *He* would act.

> **Genesis 17:1-2:** *Now when Abram was ninety-nine years old, the LORD appeared to Abram and said to him, "**I am God Almighty;** Walk before Me, and be blameless. **I will establish** My covenant between Me and you, and **I will multiply** you exceedingly." (emphasis added)*

After this, Abram had an appropriate response; he fell and *worshiped God as God.*

And then, God initiated again. He gave Abram a new identity, changing his name to "Abraham," and said He would make him a "father of nations."

> **Genesis 17:3-5: *Abram fell on his face**, and God talked with him, saying, "As for Me, behold, My covenant is with you, and you will be the father of a multitude of nations. No longer shall your name be called Abram, but **your name shall be Abraham;** For **I will** make you the father of a multitude of nations. (emphasis added)*

God continues to be the initiator in our day. We are to respond with faith in His character and worship for Him as God.

Conclusion

We were made to be in a bridal relationship with God, where we have a heart attachment to Him. He satisfies us and meets our deepest longings. Amazingly, God has designed us in such a way that experiencing His nature changes us and allows His nature to flow through us.

As we attach to Jesus and experience Him, He becomes a foundation in our soul. From this foundation comes a change in character, motivations, beliefs, thinking, and behaviors.

I hope this book has highlighted the need for an ever-deepening relationship with God. And I pray that seeing the One who is beautiful and satisfying, becomes your one thing in life. That God would become your first love and primary heart attachment.

The words of Samuel Rutherford are a fitting ending and benediction:

> *I pray that you will make prayer, and reading, and holy conference, your delight; and when delight cometh in, you shall, little by little, find the sweetness of Christ, till at length your soul be over head and ears in Christ's sweetness. Then shall you be taken up to the top of the mountain with the Lord, to know the delights of spiritual love, and the glory and excellency of a seen, revealed, felt, and embraced Christ; and then you shall not be able to loose yourself off from Christ, and to bind your soul to old lovers.*

ADDITIONAL RESOURCES

Bruce and Jean Hammond use the concepts in this book to help individuals and couples. They are available for seminars and marriage retreats, and provide online resources.

Heart
Attachment
Ministries

For more information go to www.heartattachment.com.

ENDNOTES

1 Merriam-Webster Dictionary. s.v. "epistemology." www.merriam-webster.com/dictionary/epistemology. Accessed Oct. 10, 2017.

2 Greek- "ginóskó" -1097- *Helps Word-Studies.* www.biblehub.com/greek/1097.htm. Accessed Oct. 15, 2018.

3 Greek- "epignósis", *Vines Expository Dictionary.* www.studylight.org/dictionaries/ved/k/know-known-knowledge-unknown.html Accessed Oct. 22, 2018.

4 St John of the Cross. (1990). *Dark Night Of The Soul.* New York: Doubleday, pg. 86-135.

5 Jonathan Edwards. (n.d).*Religious Affections.* [ebook]. www.jonathan-edwards.org/ReligiousAffections.pdf. Accessed Dec. 22, 2018, pg.13.

6 Ibid., pg. 9.

7 Ibid., pg. 7.

8 Greek-"gnosis." *Vines Expository Dictionary.* www.biblestudytools.com/lexicons/Greek/nas/gnosis.html. Accessed Oct. 22, 2018.

9 Greek- "epignósis." *Vines Expository Dictionary.* www.studylight.org/dictionaries/ved/k/know-known-knowledge-unknown.html. Accessed Oct. 22, 2018.

10 Richard Marks, PhD, "Are you emotionally literate enough for marriage." www.marriageworksmd.org/files/are-you-emotionally-literate-enough-for-marriage_Dr.%20Marks.pdf. Accessed Nov. 12, 2017.

ENDNOTES

11 Henry Cloud and John Townsend. (1992). *Boundaries.* Grand Rapids, MI: Zondervan Publishing House, pg.183.

12 J. Oswald Sanders. (2000). *Enjoying intimacy with God.* Grand Rapids, MI: Discovery House Publishers, pg.12.

13 Ibid., pg.126.

14 Peter Scazzero. (2006). *Emotionally Healthy Spirituality.* Nashville, TN: Integrity Publishers, Subtitle on Cover.

15 Ibid., pg.19.

16 Ravi Zacharias. "God and Pain." Ravi Zacharias International Ministries Website. www.rzim.org/read/a-slice-of-infinity/god-and-pain. Accessed Oct. 25, 2019.

17 Kendra Cherry. "Cognitive Behavioral Therapy-Process, Types, Components, Uses, and Effectiveness." (2019). www.verywellmind.com/what-is-cognitive-behavior-therapy-2795747. Accessed Aug.12, 2019.

18 Warren W. Weirsbe. *The Weirsbe Bible Commentary.* (2007).Colorado Springs, CO: David C. Cook, pg.876.

19 "understood, be wise" -4920. *Strong's Exhaustive Concordance.* www.biblehub.com/greek/4920.htm. Accessed Aug. 20, 2017.

20 C. S. Lewis. *Mere Christianity.* (1996). New York: Simon & Schuster., pg.144.

21 1 Peter 2:9. *Ellicott's Commentary.* www.biblehub.com/commentaries/ellicott/1_peter/2.htm. Assessed Mar. 21, 2016.

22 Romans 3:20. *Ellicott's Commentary.* www.biblehub.com/commentaries/ellicott/romans/3.htm. Assessed June 5, 2016.

ENDNOTES

[23] C. S. Lewis. *The Joyful Christian*. (1996). New York: Simon & Schuster, pg.138.

[24] Genesis 32:28. *Matthew Henry Commentary.* www.biblehub.com/commentaries/mhcw/genesis/32.htm. Accessed Mar. 10, 2016.

[25] Mike Bickle. *The Pleasures of Loving God*. (2000). Lake Mary, FL: Charisma House, pg.1-2.

[26] A. W. Tozer. Edited by James Snyder. *The Purpose of Man*. (2009). Ventura, CA: Regal, pg.114.

[27] John Owen. *Communion with God*. (1991). Carlisle, PA: The Banner Of Truth Trust, pg.51.

[28] Timothy Keller *Counterfeit Gods*. (2009). New York: The Penguin Group, pg.171-172.

[29] Isaiah 61. *Ellicott's Commentary.* www.biblehub.com/commentaries/ellicott/isaiah/61.htm. Accessed Jan. 5, 2016.

[30] Ephesians 4:23. *Andrew Wommack Commentary.* www.awmi.net/reading/online-bible-commentary/?bn=ephesians&cn=4&vn=23. Accessed Mar. 20, 2017.

[31] Erwin Lutzer. *Getting Closer To God*. (2000). Ann Arbor, MI: Servant Publications, pg. 186.

[32] C. S. Lewis. *The Weight of Glory and other Addresses*. (1965). Grand Rapids, MI: Eerdmans Publishing Co, pg.1-2.

[33] John Piper. *Future Grace*. (2012). Colorado Springs, CO: Multnomah Books, pg. 1.

[34] John Eldredge. *Walking With God*. (2008). Nashville, TN: Thomas Nelson, pg. 36.

ENDNOTES

[35] John Owen. *Communion with God.* (2000) Carlisle, PA: The Banner Of Truth Trust, pg. 58.

[36] E. W. Kenyon. *The Blood Covenant.* (1999). Lynnwood, WA: Kenyon's Gospel Publishing Society, pg.16.

[37] Emil Brunner. *Truth as Encounter.* (1943). Philadelphia: The Westminster Press, pg.101.

[38] Greek-"glory" 1391 *Helps Word Study.* www.biblehub.com/greek/1391.htm. Accessed Sept. 2017.

[39] By John Piper. © Desiring God Foundation. Source: desiringGod.org.

[40] A. W. Tozer. Edited by James Snyder. *The Purpose of Man.* (2009). Ventura, CA: Regal, pg.184.

[41] Philippians 3:12. *Enduring Word Commentary.* www.enduringword.com/bible-commentary/Philippians-3/. Accessed Oct. 15, 2018.

[42] J. Oswald Sanders. *Enjoying Intimacy With God.* (2000). Grand Rapids, MI: Discovery House Publishers, pg.131.

[43] Jonathan Edwards, Henry Rogers, Edward Hickman. (1839)."The Works of Jonathan Edwards, A.M., With an Essay on His Genius and Writings." https://play.google.com/books/reader?id=0bfRAAAAMAAJ&hl=en&pg=GBS.PA14. Accessed Dec. 20, 2019.

[44] Sam Storms. (2007). *Signs of the Spirit: An interpretation of Jonathan Edwards Religious Affections.* Wheaton, IL: Crossway Books, pg. 172.

[45] Ibid., pg.195.

[46] Ibid., pg.169-170.